Counseling
A Guide to Helping Others

Counseling
A Guide to Helping Others

Edited by

R. Lanier Britsch/Terrance D. Olson

Deseret Book Company
Salt Lake City, Utah

First printing in paperbound edition, March 1990

ISBN 0-87579-322-3 (v. 1)
ISBN 0-87579-323-1 (v. 2)

Library of Congress Catalog Card Number 83-72396

Printed in the United States of America

10   9   8   7   6   5   4   3   2

To JoAnn and Karen

Contents

Preface

In the fall of 1980, my wife, JoAnn, told me about a disturbing statement that had been made by one of the sisters in our ward: "If I were to walk out of my house tonight and never come back, I'd never be missed!" We decided to tell our Relief Society president about this statement. She told us that it was a symptom of a deeper problem that she and the bishop were helping to solve.

Only two days later, JoAnn learned that a friend whose husband had died about six months before was now angry with him for leaving her and their six children. She was also angry with her ward members, with her bishop, and with the Lord. When I heard about her anger, I wondered whether her bishop and her home teachers understood that she was passing through a normal stage of psychological adjustment. If she told them that she was angry, would they reply, "Oh, you don't mean that"? She did mean it! Her anger did not last long, but at the time, she meant every word. I've talked to her since, and she now looks back on her feelings with a smile.

My wife and I started thinking about the many problems people face and how great their need is for help. Almost all members of the Church find themselves at some time in the position of counselor and helper. Where can the untrained but sensitive person turn for trustworthy information? There is an abundance of excellent information available for the professional, but there is all too little information available for the lay counselor. And this is especially true of counseling information written from a Latter-day Saint point of view.

With these thoughts in mind, I began writing down topics that I knew were common problems. After talking with friends in the counseling and family relations fields, the list of topics grew even more. Everyone I mentioned the subject to expressed a need for a counseling handbook for lay counselors. Two friends in particular gave me a great deal of help in the beginning, Terrance D. Olson and Max W. Swenson. Terry later joined me as a co-editor. Max has continued to give advice and direction.

Because I knew I was unqualified to write such a book, I concluded that the best approach—and perhaps the only way the project would ever get done—was to ask qualified Latter-day Saint professionals to write chapters on various topics. Terry and I sought out competent people to handle each chapter. When we contacted these people, we found that they too believed there was a vital need for a book written by scholars for laymen about typical counseling problems. They shared our belief that lay counselors frequently found themselves in difficult situations that could be handled more intelligently and with greater inspiration if the counselors had access to basic facts about the problem at hand. We have compiled this book to explain in layman's language some of the shared wisdom of the specialists regarding a number of life's most serious and vexing problems.

We have asked professionals to write for laymen because we believe that we can "bear one another's burdens." You and I need not be professionally trained to help others, but we must operate on correct principles and have personal compassion and humility.

We have asked the authors to frame their comments in a gospel context. We have encouraged the authors to include appropriate scriptures or excerpts from General Authorities' talks. The authors have avoided jargon and technical terms. They have included examples, illustrations, and case histories. Because this is not a book for professionals, we have asked the authors to hold footnotes to a minimum.

It is not necessary to read this book from cover to cover. A reader would gain much by doing so, but each chapter stands alone.

We believe this book is valuable because a variety of authors, each with different experience, have attempted to show lay counselors a number of gospel-oriented solutions to human problems. Every author would tell you that his suggestions are a place to start, not the final solutions to the problems at hand.

This book is not a "crisis" book. It relates more to ongoing problems of adjustment in personal and family life.

This book cannot take the place of inspiration. The Lord has said, "I say unto you, that you must *study it out in your mind;* then you must ask me if it be right." (D&C 9:8.) With the Spirit's guidance, good help can be given.

The opinions expressed by the authors in this book are their own, but we would not have included them if we did not generally agree with them.

1

Introduction to Lay Counseling

R. Lanier Britsch and Terrance D. Olson

Counseling in a Church setting, whether you counsel as a neighbor, teacher, relative, friend, or Church official, is a sacred responsibility. One of the Savior's names was Counselor. To share that title is almost presumptuous of man. Nevertheless, many people find themselves in the role of counselor, even when they do not ask for the responsibility.

Many untrained counselors could be even more effective than they are if they understood some basic counseling concepts. This book provides perspectives on problems and perhaps some new attitudes that can be used to help people understand themselves. It will not teach many techniques. Through faith and inspiration, reason, and personal effort, some troubled people may be helped to overcome their problems. In a lay church like ours, many people share the burden of helping and nurturing those who have problems. Although the bishop or branch president bears a major share of the counseling burden (in many instances no one else has the authority), it is nonetheless true that many others give solace, comfort, guidance, and care. A wise bishop recently wrote, "I hear about most of the pain—spiritual, emotional, and physical—suffered by members of the ward. As a human being with all the limitations that go with being human, I cannot hope to have enough hours in the day to bind up all these wounds; consequently, I am grateful for you ward members who spontaneously have gone to the aid of your neighbors with help of all kinds."

It is unfortunate that some believe there is no place for counseling and psychology among Church members. A few even condemn all who rely on the behavioral and social sciences. We believe this rejection is wrong. Although professionals in these fields are sometimes prone to move from theory to theory or from fad to fad, behavioral and social scientists have had many valuable insights to help people overcome their problems. The concept that "Truth is truth where'er 'tis found" has meaning here.

For example, of great value to the lay counselor is the recognition that many of life's problems follow well-established patterns. Dr. Elisabeth Kübler-Ross has pointed out the stages that most people go through when they learn they have a terminal disease. If a Relief Society visiting teacher understands these stages, she can recognize symptoms of a certain stage and respond appropriately. Recognizing patterns in life, yet realizing that each situation is unique, is the beginning of wisdom.

To some people this book will look like a series of chapters designed to help nonprofessional counselors know what to do in various circumstances. And it should do just that. However, even more important than this knowledge is the moral and spiritual preparation of the counselor and of the person being helped. Sometimes both want to get on with solving the specific problem. But most specific problems are part of a larger system of problems. And, rather than merely treating symptoms, a person's capacity to meet problems is basic to solving them. The Savior said, "What manner of men ought ye to be? Verily I say unto you, even as I am." (3 Nephi 27:27.) This simple directive has been seen by some as being of no use in dealing with practical matters, or as a guilt-producing demand for perfection that is a burden, not a blessing. Mental health, spiritual growth, and solutions to everyday challenges are more permanently achieved when the counselor has the vision of becoming "even as I am" and passes that vision on to those who need help. Perhaps only then will they be able to adequately meet the trials of mortality.

Becoming like the Savior requires obedience to the gospel. Obedience is not only the first law of heaven but also the first law of mental health. Whatever suffering or conflicts we face, living by Christ's principles helps us meet challenges and solve problems. The person has the responsibility and the power to change. Helping the person accept his responsibility, and helping him realize his power to change, are fundamental to lay counseling.

Every counselor should ask himself what the Savior would do in a certain situation. There is no "right" way to counsel, but central to success is the compassion and integrity of the counselor. If you are living a lie, or if the person you are helping sees failure in your family, your effectiveness will be limited. Be sincere. Listen. Keep confidences. Share your love. Unless you have been set apart as a judge in Israel, avoid the temptation to judge. Give of your knowledge and experience as appropriate. Constantly return to the example of the Savior as you seek to give help.

Most professional counselors believe that "unconditional positive regard" for those they counsel is essential to their success. This attitude is better described as *compassionate understanding:* "Love thy neighbor as thyself."

Compassionate understanding includes the recognition that we do not counsel patients, clients, or ward members; we counsel our brothers and sisters. It also means that we are able to ache for them and to see their circumstances honestly rather than as an occasion for indifference, indulgence, or condemnation. We must offer our compassion especially when wrongdoing is a source of their predicament. This does not mean that we condone their sins or that we ignore their unwise decisions. It means that we care enough to do our best to help them. If repentance is necessary, we encourage them to repent. If forgiveness is required, we offer sincere forgiveness, if we have the authority to do so. If a lack of knowledge of gospel principles seems to be the source of their difficulties, we teach them whatever knowledge or skills we command and then, when necessary, seek help elsewhere.

Compassion is not a counseling skill; it is a way of being and a way of seeing others. It is the charity of which Paul speaks and without which we are nothing. (See 1 Corinthians 13:2.) To be a counselor is to be compassionate.

Being compassionate is not the same thing as pampering someone, however, and the compassionate counselor must place responsibility for the solution of problems on those who are seeking help. No counselor can cure the person he is helping. The troubled person must be taught or reminded that he must ultimately work out the answers to his own problems. As Abraham Lincoln observed, "You cannot build character and courage by taking away initiative and independence. You cannot help men permanently by doing for them what they could do for themselves." President David O. McKay taught, "There exists an eternal law that each human soul shall shape its own destiny. No one individual can make happiness or salvation for another."

The LDS counselor—and especially the lay counselor—will try to help people think rationally. Often people find themselves in trouble because they have unrealistic thoughts. They harbor fears, hatreds, and fantasies that have no foundation in reality. Counselors can help people with such problems revise their thinking and thus come to grips with life. Irrational thoughts lead to inappropriate emotions and behaviors.

How can a person know whether his thinking is rational, righteous, and appropriate? How do we know what is true? What is the basis for making decisions? The answers to these questions, although by no means simple, lie in a clear understanding of the gospel of Jesus Christ. Without the Savior's life as an example of correct behavior and without his teachings as a basis for decision-making, people are hard pressed to find any permanent example to follow. Contemporary philosophy is ever-changing—otherwise it would not be contemporary. As Victor L. Brown, Jr., has pointed out, *reality* is recognizing that all acts have consequences. *Illusion* is ignoring, denying, or misinterpreting consequences. Reality, then, is the recognition that all of God's laws and commands contain within themselves either good or negative results here and in the world to come.[1]

Never give counsel that is not in harmony with the principles of the gospel. No therapy or cure that is of itself immoral or inappropriate should be suggested. Correct counsel is always grounded on correct principles. Search the scriptures and other good sources. Seek the inspiration of the Lord.

Perhaps above all else, the compassionate counselor will teach faith—faith that solutions are possible, faith that time helps heal wounds, faith that the Lord Jesus Christ will share the burdens of all who lay their problems at His feet. The atonement of Jesus Christ is vital in helping people overcome their problems.

A counselor should help people understand that living according to correct principles brings more joy and happiness than does the opposite. Teaching a correct knowledge of the restored gospel is one of the lay counselor's finest tools to help troubled people understand reality.

Making Referrals

Some people with whom you counsel may not benefit from your attempts to help them. This could be due to their resistance as well as to your limitations. In any event, do not set yourself up to change the person you are counseling; you can only invite him to change, and the rest is up to him. Be open to promptings regarding the proper use of other resources with the permission and cooperation of the person you are helping. Promote the appropriate involvement of his own family members or trusted friends.

Sometimes the nature of the problem will suggest immediate referral to professionals. There is no magic formula for such referral, but you sometimes bless the person most by inviting him to seek help from experienced, trusted, and faithful professionals. Such men and women are experienced in helping people who hold extreme, even frightening attitudes. They also can ensure a regular schedule of assistance and supervision. Many professionals are willing to include religious leaders in charting a course of progress for the people you refer.

The following questions and comments might guide you in deciding when to refer someone to a professional counselor:

1. Is the person in despair? Does he insist either that life is not worth living or that he himself is worthless? The person can give up such feelings, especially when you express your own love for and confidence in the person. Nevertheless, referral may be preferable.

2. Does the person refuse to discuss within a gospel framework the problem he has presented to you? That is, do you find him discounting, ridiculing, or rejecting the gospel principles you are trying to teach? When you ask him to explain what he believes about the gospel, does he become angry? Such behavior may be typical of a "normal" person who has hardened his heart, but sometimes an angry person is doing more than venting hostility toward ward members or "just" complaining about some organizational foul-up. His resentment is more an active repudiation of what the Church stands for. In such cases, it may be important to simply ask the person, "What would you have me do?" If his answer is a more rational response about the problem, about how you can help, or about what he himself might do, then perhaps you can still offer help that will be received. If his response is not rational, professional resources may be more appropriate.

3. Does the kind of guilt harbored by the person seem to immobilize him rather than motivate him? That is, if you are teaching the person a standard of gospel behavior, is his response one of despair rather than hope? Invite him to imagine a future in which he is free of the problem. Have him describe what life would be like for him if he lived by the gospel standard in question. If he is silent for an extended period or is confused by such an invitation, referral may be appropriate. Such a question would be valuable simply to establish the depth of a person's feelings of guilt, despair, or confusion. Beware also of a response that describes the fu-

ture or the ideals in question as if they are impossible or un-realistic. Such descriptions usually reveal further that the person is immobilized by guilt precisely because he sees gospel living as impossible.

4. Does the person refuse to learn from his experiences; does he repeat errors? Does he make decisions that are not based on a realistic understanding of actions and consequences? Does he promote physical harm or in other ways threaten the well-being of others? Does he have a history of alcohol or drug use? In such cases, prayerful referral to a faithful professional may help the person.

5. Do you yourself begin to feel helpless and that the situation is hopeless? Don't spend excessive time diagnosing yourself. Invite the person to see a professional who may bring a fresh perspective to his circumstances.

You Can Help Others

A final word of encouragement: During the past hundred years counseling and psychotherapy have become almost the exclusive domain of trained professionals. Outside the Church, ministers of religion often counsel others, but most ministers refuse to counsel without some professional training. This trend has given some Church members the idea that it is impossible to give adequate counsel without professional credentials. This, of course, is not true. Counseling sometimes means nothing more than being a good friend who is willing to listen. And bishops provide good counsel simply by being in tune with the Spirit. A willingness to advise people within the bounds the Lord has set while supporting them by an outpouring of love is the key to counseling success. Non-Mormon psychiatrist M. Scott Peck has said:

> For the most part, mental illness is caused by an absence of or defect in the love that a particular child required from its particular parents for successful maturation and spiritual growth. It is obvious, then, that in order to be healed through psychotherapy the patient must receive from the psychotherapist at least a portion of the genuine love of which the patient was deprived. If the psychotherapist

cannot genuinely love a patient, genuine healing will not occur. No matter how well-credentialed and trained psychotherapists may be, if they cannot extend themselves through love to their patients, the results of their psychotherapeutic practice will be generally unsuccessful. Conversely, a totally uncredentialed and minimally trained lay therapist who exercises a great capacity to love will achieve psychotherapeutic results that equal those of the very best psychiatrists.[2]

Obviously, Dr. Peck is not calling for the dismantling of the psychotherapeutic professions. The ability to give love, backed by knowledge and experience, is clearly preferable to love alone, and as a lay counselor, you may encounter instances when you should refer a troubled person to a qualified professional. But much help can be given through direct guidance expressed in honest, loving terms. Trust the Spirit and your knowledge of God's commandments, and you will generally have success.

NOTES

1. Victor L. Brown, Jr., *Human Intimacy: Illusion and Reality* (Salt Lake City: Parliament Publishers, 1981), chapter 1.

2. M. Scott Peck, *The Road Less Traveled* (New York: Touchstone, 1978), p. 175.

ABOUT THE AUTHORS

Dr. R. Lanier (Lanny) Britsch, professor of history and coordinator of the Asian studies program at Brigham Young University, received his bachelor's and master's degrees from Brigham Young University and his Ph.D. from Claremont Graduate School.

He has served in the Church as first counselor in the Orem, Sharon Stake presidency. His previous callings include high councilor, president of the BYU Asian Students Branch, and elders quorum president.

He and his wife, JoAnn, are the parents of six children.

Dr. Terrance D. Olson, professor of family sciences at Brigham Young University, obtained degrees in sociology and family relations from that institution and his Ph.D. in marriage and family living from Florida State University.

He has spoken on strengthening the family to a subcommittee of the U.S. Senate and to sessions of the White House Conference on Families. He is a clinical member of the American Association for Marriage and Family Therapy and a member of the National Council on Family Relations.

He has served in branch and district presidencies, on high councils, as a bishop and bishop's counselor, as a Cubmaster, and on Church writing committees.

He and his wife, Karen, are the parents of six children.

2
Suffering, Pain, and Evil
R. Lanier Britsch

Although "men are that they might have joy" (2 Nephi 2:25), the world allows no one to live without a measure of pain, suffering, and sorrow. Obviously, not everyone suffers from the same problems. One observer said the root of suffering is "nothing but loneliness, isolation, solitude." If this were true of all suffering, the cure would be quite simple: draw the sufferer out of himself. However, the problem is vastly more complex. It is possible, though, to group types of suffering into three basic categories: sorrow and grief, physical pain, and guilt.

Sorrow and grief are felt by the many sufferers who have lost a loved one to death; those who have seen someone they respect or love fall from a station of self-respect because of sin, drug abuse, alcoholism, marital infidelity, or some similar indiscretion; and those who find themselves troubled with the general human condition—wars, crime, bigotry, hypocrisy, and so on. Those who suffer from physical pain make up such a large group—all mankind, really—that it is impossible to identify all the causes of pain. Whether the pain is caused by a toothache, an abscess, a tumor, a strained muscle, an eyelash, or a pin prick, the problem is real and personal.

Suffering from guilt, especially guilt caused by sin, is probably the most difficult kind of suffering to talk about or even to admit to oneself, much less to a friend, a relative, or a Church leader.

Each kind of suffering usually has a cure, and some of the cures are actually easy to prescribe. The cure for suffering caused by guilt from sin is repentance, which is easily recommended but seldom easily done. The cure for physical pain is to heal the source of the pain, which is usually disease. Often, healing the body includes restoring psychological health as well. Physical illnesses are frequently related to family, social, and employment problems.

No theological or philosophical issue has caused Christians more trouble than that of suffering, pain, and evil. "How can you believe in the goodness of God," someone asks, "when there is so much evil in the world?" Newspaper headlines seem to cry out in witness against the goodness and mercy of God: "One hundred thousand die in Bangladesh cyclone"; "Several millions starving in Africa"; "Five pedestrians killed by deranged woman in Reno." "How," the skeptic asks, "can you account for such a world?"

The restored gospel gives better answers to these questions than does any other religion or philosophy. God is the father of our spirits. We lived with him in his celestial realm before we came here, and he explained the purpose of our existence and the necessity of living away from him for a time. We were to gain physical bodies and to be tested to see how well we would live by faith. We were given freedom of choice, and our choices would determine whether or not we would someday return to our Father, having learned to be like him. Because of the improper choices of ourselves and others, we would suffer pain, sorrow, evil, and tribulations of all kinds. But to those of us who understood God's plan, it was plain that we could not grow and progress without agency and its results. To remove the consequences of our sins and mistakes would be to destroy agency itself, and thus any progress we might make.

Try to imagine a world without a negative side, a world without hunger and sickness, without failure and disappointment, without injustice, hatred, oppression, and death. Such a world would be devoid of spiritual strength, growth, adventure, zest. It would be a world without compassion, courage, helpfulness, hope, integrity, love. In Henry Thomas's words, "Evil, then, is a hurdle for the exercise of the muscles of the soul. Good is not the *absence* of evil. It is the active and incessant *advancement against evil.*" Suffering, pain, and evil must be allowed their influences. Without them we could never enjoy their opposites.

Just as some people misunderstand the need for the negative side of life, others misinterpret the word *love*, especially when it is applied to God. The scriptures say that God is love. (1 John 4:8.) But certainly that is not *all* God is. Indeed, the Lord chastens those whom he loves. (Hebrews 12:6.) He chastened even the Savior himself: "Though he were a Son, yet learned he obedience by the things which he suffered." (Hebrews 5:8.) We err if we think God's sole purpose is to give us comfort. Consider C. S. Lewis's view: "We want, in fact, not so much a Father in Heaven as a grandfather in heaven—a senile benevolence who, as they say, 'liked to see young people enjoying themselves,' and whose plan for the universe was simply that it might be truly said at the end of each day, 'a good time was had by all.'"[1] Latter-day Saints do not believe in such a God. Our God expects work, progress, effort, and every other good quality. He wants us to grow through experience.

Sometimes Church members are shocked when a young missionary dies. "Why would God allow such a thing?" they ask. Reflection would bring to mind the sufferings and death of both the Savior and of Joseph Smith. Righteousness in no way assures one of physical or mental comfort. All hell raged against the Prophet Joseph while he was in Liberty Jail. After recounting a catalog of evils, persecutions, and suffering— seemingly more than any mortal could bear—the Lord said to Joseph: "Know thou, my son, that all these things shall give thee *experience*, and shall be for thy good." (D&C 122:7; italics added.) Herein lies an important principle: The Lord cares about our reactions, our attitudes toward suffering, pain, and sorrow. The specific circumstances or conditions do not matter much. God allows the world to have its way. The issue is how we react to the world.

Knowing this, however, does not shut off the pain when we hurt. Sometimes pain is so constant it can impede or impair "the sufferer's ability to work and to think clearly, [and] prevents his sleep, abolishes appetite, lowers morale, and may even destroy his will to help himself survive."[2] When pain is severe, you as a counselor should make sure the person has received adequate medical attention and that appropriate prayers have been said and priesthood blessings administered. (See D&C 42:48.) You should also consider the person's environment and way of life. Pain is not always caused by physical problems. "Some recent evidence," writes David Bakan, "suggests that disease may be conceived of as a manifestation of a deeper disorder involving the total condition of the individual and that a specific disease from which any individual appears to be suffering may be regarded as its manifestation."[3] Dr. Hans Selye, in the *Stress of Life*, suggests that behind the obvious causes of pain or disease are other causes not so obvious:

> If a man is hit over the head with the club of a policeman and suffers permanent brain damage from the injury, it seems rather obvious that his disease was caused by the club. But if you come to think of it, the blow was not the real first cause; it was but one link in the sequence of a chain-reaction that eventually led to brain injury. What actually happened may have been that the officer asked the man not to loiter, whereupon the latter reacted violently insulting and assailing the policeman, who in turn hit him over the head with the club. So, in fact, the principle, immediate cause of the man's injury was his own unwarranted, aggressive behavior.[4]

Such reasoning raises many questions. Are we not the cause of many of our diseases and pains? If we are overweight, if we fail to exercise, if we eat too much, if we fail to get enough sleep (or get too much sleep), if we don't drive safely, if we smoke, if we drink alcoholic beverages, or if we use drugs unwisely, who is to blame for the pain and disease that follow? If we work in unhealthy, stressful, or dangerous conditions, are we not to some degree responsible for the negative consquences? If our families are unhappy because of our selfishness or lack of concern, are we not creating the conditions that will ultimately bring us pain and sorrow? Clearly, counselors are responsible to advise behavior changes to solve problems. For example, most of us have friends who are dangerously overweight. They have shortness of breath, high blood pressure, fatigue, and low self-esteem. Such people usually need help beyond what we can give as friends. Competent medical or psychological help (or both) should be advised in a direct but kind manner.

Although we often cause many of our own problems, it is a mistake to condemn ourselves or a suffering friend and conclude that the Lord is inflicting suffering and pain as a punishment for sins. We've all heard people say that if someone had not sinned, he would not be undergoing trials and suffering. As friends and advisers, we have no right to judge others. (Bishops and stake presidents, of course, have the calling to judge, but the rest of us do not.) Consider Joseph Smith's counsel: "It is a false idea that the Saints will escape all the judgments, whilst the wicked suffer; for all flesh is subject to suffer. . . . So that it is an unhallowed principle to say that such and such have transgressed because they have been preyed upon by disease or death, for all flesh is subject to death; and the Savior has said, 'Judge not, lest ye be judged.' "[5]

It is best to help a suffering person know he is loved of God and that the Lord is mindful of all who suffer: "All things wherewith you have been afflicted shall work together for your good, and to my name's glory, saith the Lord." (D&C 98:3.)

Sorrow and grief are some of the most difficult problems to help people overcome. The key to helping is to provide a broader perspective of the problem. If mortality were the whole of existence, pain, sorrow, failure, and seeming inequities would be a calamity. But the larger view helps us to know that there is never any loss without a new beginning. Several years ago I lost a dear friend and several of his family members in a plane crash. My friend was gone, but another mutual friend who also loved the departed redoubled his efforts to live righteously. As President Kimball has said, "there is no tragedy in death, but only in sin."[6] "We cannot always understand the plans of the Almighty," wrote Elder Melvin J. Ballard, "but I feel sure that He does all things well and that sometimes the thing that seems almost like a disaster is a blessing in disguise. The only thing that matters is that we keep the right attitude. It is only when we become bitter that we let it change our whole lives, but when we can keep our courage and keep our eyes upon the mark and still go on toward our destiny, that is what matters. All these trials become purifying influences in our lives and leave us purer gold by and by."[7]

For those who sorrow and grieve because of the iniquities and failings of other men, the best help is to remind them of the positive side of life and that God is just in all his dealings with mankind. We will be judged for our own sins and not for Adam's transgression. Nor must we be *overly* sorrowful for the sins of others, even the sins of close relatives. Sorrow should bring us to action. It should teach us the bounds of human endurance. It should motivate us to love others who have fallen. Sorrow for sinners should remind us of our own shortcomings and failings, but too much sorrow is debilitating and will impede our progress and impair our spiritual health.

Although those who suffer sometimes resist seeing anything worthwhile in life, it is, nevertheless, basic to their recovery that they recognize the positive. Courage to see advantages and gains rather than disadvantages and drawbacks will help relieve fears and tensions and create a calmer atmosphere in which to live. The Lord does not expect us to give in to pain and suffering or to be fatalistic and resigned to it. Man has an obligation to battle the negative side effects of his mortal environment.

Courage is based on spiritual conviction. And spiritual conviction cannot be turned on like tap water. It is more like a deep well or an underground stream. During an unusually severe drought, when even the canals are dried and parched, the first trees to die are not those on the plains, but the lush, healthy ones that grow along the canals. Why? Because the trees on the flat, hot countryside have of necessity put down deeper and deeper roots over the years. The trees by the canals have had no need to stretch deep to survive. Without resources, they are the first to die. In a similar manner, people who do not have deep spiritual roots, convictions, and courage will have a difficult time adjusting in times of crisis. There is value in helping a troubled friend prepare now for future crises. Life will bring sudden reversals. Help your suffering loved one to decide now his reactions to future difficulties. Imagining how he will handle a problem the next time it occurs can create emotional stability.

Children, too, should be helped to recognize that misfortune befalls everyone. Those who are shielded from problems will seldom be aware of the misfortunes of others. Nor will they be aware of their own vulnerability in life. Like plants raised in a hothouse where the temperature never varies, they will have a hard time adjusting to the fluctuations of the real world. To those who have not known pain, pain seems unjust when it strikes. But pain and sorrow have nothing to do with justice. Our ability to cope rests on how realistically we face the inevitable suffering life brings us. Trials can help us develop tenderness, gentleness, and greater competence to deal with life.

Certainly it is unwise to seek trouble. But neither should we be afraid to confront and deal with reality. Contemporary customs so diminish the impact of death, childbirth, and many other special and sacred moments that their meaning is often lost. George Wald, a Nobel Prize winner, thoughtfully wrote, "Just realize, I am 69 and I have never seen a person die. I have never even been in the same house while a person died. How about birth? An obstetrician invited me to see my first birth only last year. Just think, these are the greatest events of life and they have been taken out of our experience. We somehow hope to live full emotional lives when we have carefully expunged the sources of the deepest human emotions. When you have no experience of pain, it is rather hard to experience joy."[8] People should be helped to realize that some of life's sweetest moments accompany those events that are most difficult to face.

Many people try to get through their problems alone. But

a key to being healed is to accept help from friends and loved ones. And if a sufferer listens to others, he will find that he does not suffer alone. Suffering and sorrow also diminish when the sufferer does something for someone else.

Sin is the one cause of suffering over which we have control. The world has attempted to deny its existence. Psychologists have sometimes substituted the word *symptom* for *sin*. Freudians have sometimes attempted to rid their patients of guilt feelings by telling them there is no such thing as sin. Nevertheless, sin is real.

There is no need to catalog the multitude of sins. It is enough to say that when a person is suffering because he has sinned, the cure is repentance. But those who suffer should be sure their sins are real. Some Church members may suffer needlessly because of imagined offenses or because of the overzealousness of a few well-meaning but thoughtless people. Frequently, young mothers are exhausted with the struggle to remain solvent on a meager budget, to keep several youngsters clean and fed, and to carry on the duties of Churchworker and wife all at the same time. Counselors might read Ecclesiastes 3:1 with concerned young mothers: "To everything there is a season, and a time to every purpose under the heaven."

But if sins are real, you may be able to help your friend muster the courage to repent. You can also be of great help if you review the meaning of the atonement of Jesus Christ. Church leaders occasionally meet with a member who has read Doctrine and Covenants 1:31: "For I the Lord cannot look upon sin with the least degree of allowance." But the member either forgets to read or refuses to see the next verse: "Nevertheless, he that repents and does the commandments of the Lord shall be forgiven." It is often harder to forgive ourselves than to forgive others. We tend to demand more of ourselves. In fact, we sometimes look at the best qualities of our five or ten best friends and wonder why we do not have all of them. Help your troubled friend evaluate the nature of his sins (as far as is appropriate if you are not a bishop, branch president, or other authorized Church leader), understand the steps of repentance, have faith in the Atonement, and forgive himself.

Regardless of the source of suffering, the most important thing you can do to help is to be a true friend. You must share the grief, the pain, the sorrow. But in some instances you must make it gently clear that the problem belongs to the person who is suffering. Only he, with the help of the Lord, can finally recover wholeness and emotional stability. As a counselor, you can do much to help your friend know that he is loved and of value. Few things are more important.

NOTES

1. C. S. Lewis, *The Problem of Pain* (New York: Macmillan Publishing Co., 1962), p. 40.

2. J. C. White and W. H. Sweet, *Pain: Its Mechanisms and Neurosurgical Control* (Springfield, Ill.: Charles C. Thomas, 1955), p. 99.

3. David Bakan, *Disease, Pain, and Sacrifice: Toward a Psychology of Suffering* (Chicago and London: University of Chicago Press, 1968), p. 13.

4. Hans Selye, *The Stress of Life* (New York: McGraw-Hill Book Co., 1956), pp. 128-29.

5. Joseph Smith, *History of The Church of Jesus Christ of Latter-day Saints*, 7 vols., 2nd ed. rev., edited by B. H. Roberts (Salt Lake City: The Church of Jesus Christ of Latter-day Saints, 1948) 4:11.

6. Spencer W. Kimball, *Faith Precedes the Miracle* (Salt Lake City: Deseret Book Co. 1972), p. 101.

7. Melvin R. Ballard, comp.,*Melvin J. Ballard . . . Crusader for Righteousness* (Salt Lake City: Bookcraft, 1967), p. 275.

8. Philip Yancey, *Where Is God When It Hurts?* (Grand Rapids: Zondervan Publishing House, 1977), p. 41.

SUGGESTED READINGS

Jack S. Bailey, *Let Not Your Heart Be Troubled: Answers to Problems of Human Suffering* (Bountiful, Utah: Horizon Publishers, 1976).

Spencer W. Kimball, "Death—Tragedy or Destiny," in *Faith Precedes the Miracle* (Salt Lake City: Deseret Book Co., 1972).

Philip Yancey, *Where Is God When It Hurts?* (Grand Rapids: Zondervan Publishing House, 1977).

3

Crisis Intervention
Richard D. Berrett

The phone rings several times before Bishop Cole, with eyes still closed and senses dulled by sleep, finds it and places the receiver to his ear. Through muffled sobs, a woman relates the details of an evening of fighting with her husband: caustic remarks, painful accusations, bitter confrontations—a crisis.

The silence settling on the emergency room brings with it the realization that the baby is dead. The medical staff did all they could. Still, the baby is gone. Numbed, the parents stare blankly at the wall. They seem to be in another world, the world of crisis.

Answering the knock at the door, a youth leader sees an angry teenager desperate to tell his story: "Mom and Dad just don't understand me. They won't listen. I hate them!" A crisis.

Each of these situations illustrates the overwhelming nature of a crisis. The people involved feel helpless because their problems seem to have no solutions—they lack the necessary resources to cope with their difficulties.

Individuals and families constantly adjust to the demands of life. These adjustments usually provide people with a sense of security. But when a person finds adjusting too difficult, he may develop a sense of helplessness and inability to cope. Crisis intervention includes helping people who are unable to adjust to the challenges of life to regain the sense of stability and security that they enjoyed prior to the crisis.

Some people, because of past experiences, are more resilient to the shock of a crisis and may require little aid. Others who are less experienced and who may lack the necessary resources often demand immediate help. You can help by understanding the crisis, by exploring available resources, and by evaluating possible solutions and their consequences with the person.

Understanding the Crisis

The first help a lay counselor can give is to offer a listening ear and a comforting voice. As the troubled person expresses his feelings to someone who is nonjudgmental, calm, interested, empathetic, and helpful, his stress diminishes, and he gains a more realistic understanding of his crisis. Here is an example of such a discussion:

Stacie: Bishop Cole, Jim left about an hour ago, and I know he doesn't love me anymore. How could he walk out on me and the children?

Bishop: It seems to you that if he really cared he wouldn't have left?

Stacie: Yes, I could have left too; after all, I'm the one who is rejected, not him.

Bishop: You sound as if you don't think Jim is hurt by what has happened.

Stacie: If it did hurt him, he sure didn't let me know.

Bishop: Could it be that when Jim is really hurt, he becomes angry and leaves? Maybe his leaving doesn't mean he no longer loves you and the children, but that he is so frustrated he doesn't know what else to do.

Stacie: I hadn't thought of it that way.

Through listening carefully to Stacie, reflecting her emotions and thoughts back to her, and asking relevant questions, the bishop helps her understand the crisis. He helps her distinguish her feelings about the crisis from the actual nature of the crisis. After all, it is possible that Jim left feeling as much pain as Stacie and that Stacie's belief that he doesn't love her is incorrect.

When you, the counselor, gain an accurate view of the nature of the crisis, you become a source of understanding and information for the person you counsel. The trust you build as you demonstrate concern by listening will influence the person to listen to your guidance. He will become more willing to explore all parts and implications of the crisis and to receive your counsel. You should clarify, give perspective, and define the crisis so that the sufferer's anxiety is reduced and his hope is rekindled.

Avoid simple prescriptions. If you give simple prescriptions without really listening to the person, he will become defensive and may reject your recommendations. Your effectiveness as a counselor is based on your ability to demonstrate understanding and concern.

It is important in a crisis to assess the person's stability. Because the crisis may leave him helpless and hopeless, he may consider suicide. It is wise to discuss with the person whether he has suicidal thoughts. Facing such thoughts head-on can prevent a suicide. Similarly, finding out whether the distressed person has violent feelings toward others may keep him from harming someone else. If the danger is great enough that your discussion does not decrease his hatred and rage, it may be essential to seek professional aid.

Discussing several questions with those going through a crisis can help them understand the crisis. You might ask: What caused the crisis? How are others being affected by the experience? Has this type of thing occurred before? How long has this been happening? Who else knows about the trouble?

After the troubled person and the counselor understand the crisis, the second phase of crisis intervention may begin.

Using Appropriate Resources

Because of the urgency of a crisis, it is generally necessary to give immediate help to alleviate it. Several sources of help are available, and it is important for the counselor to use each one that is appropriate. These sources are discussed below:

Spiritual Strength

Religious beliefs provide an eternal perspective for many of life's tragedies. The counselor can help people explore the broad meanings of discouraging experiences. Marital difficulty might be seen as a chance to develop a stronger marriage through greater effort. Death might promote a desire to live worthy of a reunion with the deceased. Family conflict can indicate the need to increase family time together and to improve family communication.

The power of prayer and fasting often helps those who are troubled. And many testify of the comfort they have felt as a group of concerned friends united in prayer and fasting on their behalf. In some circumstances a special blessing might be administered to one who is suffering. A message of consolation from the Lord through those giving blessings often lifts the troubled. Counselors should seek spiritual guidance in crisis situations and should encourage those they are helping to seek the power of spiritual resources.

Personal Worth

Unfortunately, many people interpret a crisis as an indication that they lack personal worth. If they are troubled and overwhelmed, they feel weak, inadequate, or even worthless. It is important for the troubled person to build his self-esteem. Questions that provide insight into the person's strengths will help him do this: Have you made it through difficult periods before? What have you done in the past to help when things seemed overwhelming? What strengths do you have that might help you solve this problem? As a more balanced picture of one's power to deal with difficulties emerges from such discussions, the person will become aware of himself as a resource. This can provide confidence that the crisis will pass and that he can solve his problems.

The Chinese character for crisis suggests both danger and opportunity. Quite naturally, in the early stages of crisis, one is most aware of the dangers involved. But as a person explores his strengths, he becomes more sensitive to the opportunities that may be present. Enhancing self-worth by overcoming adversity is one such opportunity. Effective counselors help people see themselves as part of the solution to the crisis.

The Family

Families are too often deprived of the chance to become closer through supporting one another during traumatic periods. Counselors can help a person overcome his pride and fears by exploring the resources of his immediate and extended family. You might ask: Who do you trust the most in your family? Would you be willing to let me ask for their help? If they were in a similar circumstance, would you be eager to help them? Could it be that your pride is interfering with your willingness to seek their help?

Families can and should offer emotional support during the most trying of times. For example, a sick child requires help beyond the abilities of the working parents. The child's aunt is a resource who may come as an "angel of mercy" to care for the sick child. If a person can't pay a utility bill, a financially secure cousin might be called upon for help. A family forced to evacuate their home because of flood danger, might move in with the husband's sister. Counselors should help people explore all possible family resources that may help them solve their problems.

The Church

The Church has extensive resources to help with crises. These resources, with plans for their use, are outlined in various Church handbooks. The resources include "commodities, fast offering funds, job opportunities, and services provided by LDS Social Services or Deseret Industries, welfare services missionaries, welfare service committee members, and Church members with specific skills and resources."[1] After identifying the nature of the crisis, the counselor may

use the appropriate resources available through the Church
to help the troubled person.

The Community.
  The Church's *Welfare Services Resource Handbook*
notes, "Community resources that provide services consistent with Church standards may be used. These include
family counseling centers, clinics for the handicapped, private counselors or therapists, alcohol or drug rehabilitation
centers, university medical centers, mental hospitals, outpatient clinics, and extended care facilities. State agencies,
including agricultural extension services, and private
professional persons, including psychologists, education
counselors, agronomists, accountants, attorneys, and doc-
tors, should be evaluated and approved by the bishop before
their services are used. The bishop should help members determine how they can receive such assistance without fear of
ridicule or pressure to change values (such as values con-
nected with Church positions on chastity, abortion, marriage, family prayer, church activity, and the Word of Wisdom)."[2]

Using the Resources Available
  Effective counselors will use these resources to help in
crisis situations. The following example illustrates these
principles.

> The Hill family was in a state of shock when their home teacher
> arrived at the hospital emergency room. Annette, their four-year-old
> and youngest in the family, had been hit by a car. After being rushed
> to the hospital, she died. Several days passed before the shock sub-
> sided and the reality hit the family members. Brother Hill withdrew
> from contact with almost all his friends. He was unable to work be-
> cause of his intense emotions over his daughter's death. He would
> often lock himself in his room for long periods of time. The crisis of
> Annette's death was now compounded by the reaction of her father.
>   Through delicate discussions with Brother Hill, his home teacher
> discovered Brother Hill's deep feelings of guilt about his daughter's
> death. The home teacher determined that the depressed feelings re-
> sulted from the idea that in some way Brother Hill had caused his

daughter's death. He reported coming home later than usual the day of the accident and not spending his accustomed playtime with Annette. He felt that if he had been home earlier, she would have come home from her friend's house before the traffic increased and would not have been hit.

During the next several weeks, the home teacher and Brother Hill talked almost daily. These discussions revealed that although Brother Hill was seriously depressed, he was not considering suicide and could begin to examine the crisis in a broader, more realistic way. The home teacher's goals included helping Brother Hill through his intense guilt, helping him reestablish contact with those from whom he was isolated, and helping him develop the emotional strength to cope with this experience for which he was totally unprepared.

During this period, Brother Hill fasted and prayed often, and this helped him greatly. Blessing his wife and children gave him renewed contact with his family and an opportunity to think of the other family members during this crisis that affected all of them.

Soon he returned to work and was surprised by the concern and support received from his co-workers. His supervisors, too, seemed to reach out with understanding toward him.

Brother Hill also took time to study death. He read several books about how others have coped with losing loved ones and discovered he was not alone in his experience. Through study, he also began to develop an eternal perspective about death, which helped him move from a feeling of hopelessness to one of hope. Brother Hill learned to understand his guilt feelings and that they would pass.

In this example, the troubled person at first saw the accident as his responsibility. He withdrew from contact with his family, friends, and others who might be sources of support. Because of his incorrect ideas and actions, he increased his stress and the seriousness of the crisis. Later, however, he used appropriate resources to help him understand the crisis and overcome his problems. Some of the resources he used were spiritual strength, his family, and the Church. Counselors should always encourage the troubled people who come to them to use such resources.

Evaluating Possible Solutions and Their Consequences

After defining the crisis and examining the available resources, the counselor and the troubled person should examine possible solutions to the problem. An important part of doing this is considering the possible consequences of each solution. After they have discussed several solutions, the counselor and the person should choose the solution that will best solve the problem and try it to see if it works. It would be wise to seek the Lord's help in doing this.

As you read the following dialogue, notice how the counselor helps solve the crisis by (1) helping the troubled person understand it, (2) exploring available resources, and (3) evaluating possible solutions and their consequences.

Dave:	Mom and Dad don't understand me. They won't even listen. I hate them!
Counselor:	Will you tell me what happened, Dave?
Dave:	They say I can't take the car to the dance on Saturday because I didn't go to church last week. And they say if I don't do better in school, I'll be grounded for the rest of the term.
Counselor:	You seem to think your parents have made some really hard demands on you.
Dave:	Wow, is that an understatement! They're just crazy, and I don't care if I ever see them again.
Counselor:	I guess you'd like to hurt them because they're causing so much trouble for you.
Dave:	That's right, I'd like to tell them what I really think of them.
Counselor:	Would that help you feel better about not having the car on Saturday?
Dave:	No, not really, but at least it would let them share some of the problems they're giving me.
Counselor:	This may sound like something your mom and dad would say, but I hope you'll understand I'm just trying to help you solve this problem. Could it be they're already hurt because you're not doing as well as they think you can in school and aren't going to church with them?
Dave:	Yeah, I know they don't like what's going on.
Counselor:	Why don't we jump in the car and go talk with them about these problems?
Dave:	No thanks. I never want to see them again.
Counselor:	Is not seeing them another way to pay them back for what they have done?

Dave:	That's right.
Counselor:	Well, how will not seeing them solve the problem about the car?
Dave:	It won't.
Counselor:	Maybe since they have control of the car and they are the ones you are having trouble with, they are the most important resources you have to solve these problems.
Dave:	But how do you talk to someone you hate?
Counselor:	Have you hated them in the past?
Dave:	Yes.
Counselor:	Did you stop after the problem became less serious?
Dave:	Yeah, I did.
Counselor:	Well, if you stopped hating them over problems in the past, maybe trying to solve this problem with their help might help you stop hating them now.
Dave:	Maybe, but what about the car for Saturday?
Counselor:	Let's go over there and talk with them, and maybe your anger and having the car can be worked out.
Dave:	Okay.

Notice how the counselor in this example helped his friend understand his problem. Dave realized that his anger was only temporary because of the car, that he did not really hate his parents. The counselor also suggested an appropriate resource to help solve the problem: Dave's parents. Finally, the counselor helped Dave explore possible solutions and their consequences, and they decided to try one of the solutions.

Suicide

Perhaps the most serious crisis is a potential suicide. Successful prevention is more likely when a lay counselor recognizes some of the elements of suicide attempts. Generally, the person contemplating suicide is faced with a problem he believes is unsolvable and intolerable. His feelings of helplessness and despair create stress, depression, and withdrawal from all who could give support. Appetite is frequently depressed, causing a weight loss. Often, the person doesn't sleep well, and may awake in the middle of the night and be unable to get back to sleep.

Such symptoms may result from a severe loss of some

type, such as a loved one's death, a broken relationship, un-employment, or a loss of self-esteem.

Counselors who are aware of these situations and symptoms need to become extremely sensitive to words and actions that may indicate thoughts of suicide. Such state-ments as "I don't know how I can go on without her," "Things really don't matter anymore," or "Soon everything will be taken care of, and nobody will have to worry any longer" may suggest a preparation for suicide. Changing one's will, taking out a large insurance policy, giving away valued objects, quitting school or a job, or breaking off contact with friends and relatives may be steps toward suicide.

Suicide attempts are often a cry for help. The victim, feel-ing unable to cope with his problems, thinks about suicide, talks about suicide, and attempts suicide. *It is not true that those who talk about taking their lives will never do it.* Such talk may lead to action unless someone intercedes.

The seriousness of the risk can be gauged by the person's circumstances. Does the person have a gun, lots of sleeping pills, or access to an automobile? Generally the more specific the threats and the more lethal the method he has in mind, the greater likelihood of a suicide attempt.

When anyone threatens directly or subtly to take his life, even in jest, you should start looking for other signs of con-templated suicide.

It is crucial that you contact a professional if it appears there is some possibility of suicide. It would be far better to contact a professional and find a suicide threat to be a false alarm than to think you are overreacting to a threat and delay until it is too late.

The person you think has suicidal feelings needs to know that you care about him, that you have some ideas about how to help him solve his problems, and that there is hope for the future. Helping the person plan a better future is one way to show him that help is available. Moreover, a discus-sion of alternative future plans helps him see that things need not be hopeless.

It may be necessary to talk about how suicide would be futile while other alternatives would not be. Since a person contemplating suicide often thinks living is futile, you should show him that just the opposite is true. Where there is life, there is hope, but suicide will only intensify any problems that already exist. By discussing opportunities available to the person by choosing to *live*, and by showing him that he would cheat himself of those opportunities if he chose to die, you may be able to decrease his desire to die.

Of course, these suggestions assume that the person will talk rationally with you. Even if the person is not rational or doesn't feel your suggestions are meaningful, keep talking. To help yourself do this, ask yourself: What does my love of this person require of me? How can I communicate my concern? Even if his life seems to mean nothing to him, how can I teach him that his life has meaning to me?

Summary

Helping people in crisis is one of the most difficult tasks a counselor faces, as well as one of the most rewarding. Helping people grow from emotional helplessness and hopelessness into confidence and strength is the very essence of gospel service.

NOTES

1. *Welfare Services Resource Handbook* (Salt Lake City: The Church of Jesus Christ of Latter-day Saints, 1980), p. 22.

2. Ibid., p. 23.

ABOUT THE AUTHOR

Dr. Richard D. Berrett, professor of child and family studies at California State University at Fresno, received his bachelor's and master's degrees from Brigham Young University and his Ph.D. from Florida State University. A member of many national and regional professional and honorary societies, Professor Berrett is a past president of the Association of Mormon Counselors and Psychotherapists. He is a clinical member of the American Association for Marriage and Family Therapy. In addition to his teaching and research responsibilities, he is in private practice in marriage, family, and child therapy.

An active member of the Church, Dr. Berrett has served in a Young Men presidency, as a ward executive secretary, as a full-time missionary, and on district and stake high councils.

He and his wife, Christine, are the parents of three children.

4
Depression
David G. Weight

Abraham Lincoln, who struggled with depression throughout much of his life, once wrote, "If what I feel were equally distributed to the whole human family, there would not be one cheerful face on earth." Depression takes an inestimable toll on the human family, and it is the most common complaint brought to the attention of professional and lay counselors alike. The condition might be thought of as the "common cold" of emotional problems, since it occurs so broadly, is found with so many other physical and mental disorders, and is difficult to cure. According to the National Institute of Mental Health, at least 15 percent of all adults between the ages of eighteen and seventy-four suffer the destructive effects of depression sometime. The actual incidence, however, may be much higher, estimated as high as 30 percent. Estimates of dollar costs for this disorder have been placed at between 300 and 900 million dollars. As a counselor, friend, or relative of a depressed person, you should quickly recognize how devastating this condition can be to the person as well as to his family and friends. And since suicide is often considered by the depressed person as the solution to his despair and self-condemnation, this condition may be dangerous enough to require professional treatment.

Signs of Depression

Everyone has changes in mood from time to time. Negative moods seldom last for more than a few days, and a person would rarely seek help from a counselor in such cases. These "normal" depressions are usually related to stress, disappointment, or even biological change. In many cases, grieving at the loss of a loved one or an important relationship will produce short-term depression. Short-term counseling in adjusting to these mood swings may be helpful, and it may avoid the development of deeper depression. Our greater concerns, however, are for those whose depression stays relatively unchanged for longer than a week or two.

According to Aaron Beck,[1] depression has four major facets: emotional, cognitive, motivational, and physical.

Emotional

The depressed person usually has pronounced feelings of hopelessness and despair with periods of uncontrolled crying and feelings of guilt and unworthiness. The person will often describe awakening in the morning and feeling a kind of gloominess settle around him. He may feel that even the most basic requirements of life are overwhelming and frightening. Such a person often feels tension and anxiety and finds it difficult to think and concentrate. He may also feel a loss of control and be troubled by fear of insanity, disease, or even death. Perhaps the most characteristic emotional symptom of depression, however, is the person's loss of interest or pleasure in almost all of his usual activities and pastimes. Nothing seems worth doing. In fact, the severely depressed individual may have almost no sense of love, excitement, or accomplishment.

Most depressed people feel guilty. They often believe that their behavior is sinful and that their depressive feelings may be God's punishment. They may believe they have committed an unpardonable sin or have been abandoned by God. In extreme cases this feeling may be psychotic.[2] The counselor will have to evaluate whether such guilt is justified while recognizing that guilt is often a symptom of depression.

Some people do not experience guilt, but blame their depression on external causes. They may believe that if the counselor or others would reduce their demands, the depression would leave.

Cognitive

Some depressed people experience poor concentration, memory problems, difficulty in carrying on a normal conversation, and preoccupation with the fear of looking foolish. They have great difficulty making decisions or being creative. Unfortunately, these reactions feed the person's feeling of inadequacy and incompetence, which produce greater difficulty in performance and production, which leads to increased feelings of incompetence, and so on, dragging the person into a downward cycle of despair.

Motivational

Everything seems difficult to depressed people. Morning seems to be the worst time of the day, since the effort required to get up and get going seems so monumental. They are afraid to encounter other people or their usual work, since they will be reminded of their failure and inadequacy. They often cut back on social activities and stay home for long periods of time, sometimes in bed. They have little ambition to take on new projects, and church or work obligations seem overwhelming.

Physical

During depression, the body often exhibits what are known as the *"clinical signs of depression."* These include sleep disturbances, eating disturbances, decrease in sexual drive, and loss of physical energy.

Sleep disturbances. Depressed people may have a difficult time falling asleep or may awaken early in the morning and not be able to get back to sleep. However, they may also require more and more sleep, wanting to spend every available moment in bed.

Eating disturbances. Those who are depressed may lose their appetites and experience rapid weight loss. They may describe eating as something that is done only because it is necessary, and they may get little pleasure from eating. On the other hand, they may develop voracious appetites with nervous and sporadic eating throughout the day. Constipation and gastrointestinal problems are also typical.

Decrease in sexual drive. With a general decrease in the capacity for pleasure, depressed people often report reduced sexual interest. In severe cases, the body temporarily loses its capacity for sexual excitement.

Loss of physical energy. Depressed people often report fatigue and loss of energy. In extreme cases, it is difficult for them even to move about the house. Coordination between the mind and the body may slow to such a point that reaction time is impaired, and the people may have difficulty with tasks they usually do well. They may also feel agitated with constant need to pace and to rub their hands, hair, skin, clothing, or other objects. They usually speak very little and seem tired even without any physical exertion. They may also report having pain when there is no medical explanation for it.

Depression in Children

Depression in children can be difficult to recognize. Since younger children do not have a well-developed ability to think or talk about abstract concepts, a counselor must look for behavioral clues to a child's depression. A gloomy mood or failure to find excitement in life are signs of depression. The child may withdraw from other children, fail to gain weight, or develop a clinging and insecure attachment to parents or other adults. Adolescent boys may develop anti-social behavior and feel misunderstood and rejected. Girls may become sexually promiscuous in an attempt to be accepted by others. Withdrawal from social activities, reluctance to attend family outings, and spending increasing amounts of time alone are also signs of depression. Other signs include difficulty with schoolwork, inattention to personal appearance, and overly strong reactions to love relationships. The adolescent, of course, is much more able to think about and discuss depression than can young children, and they can contribute more to their own treatment.

Medical Causes of Depression

Depression can be caused by medical problems, such as untreated diabetes, side effects from medications, or changes in the brain from stroke or senility. Because this is true, if depression lasts longer than a week or two, the person should see a medical doctor. If the doctor finds no medical cause for the depression, the person should probably be referred to a mental health professional.

Counseling the Depressed

Even if the depressed person is seeing a mental health professional, the lay counselor can do much to help him (being sure, of course, not to undermine the work of the professional). First, it is important that the counselor establish a relationship with the person that will inspire confidence. Depressed people often feel they are disclosing frightening and terrible aspects of themselves and are afraid that other people would take advantage of this information and tell it to their neighbors, ward members, and others. Establishing confidentiality and confidence is vital to helping those who are depressed.

The counselor must also attempt to understand the person's despair. Sometimes a *counselor* has had depressed feelings and would like to deny the existence of depression in other people to protect himself from his own feelings. This is particularly true of one counseling a member of his own family. We love people in our families, want them to be successful, and want to help them take responsibility for their emotional problems. However, we may deny the existence or severity of their depression. Remember, one reason a person seeks out a counselor or confidant is to find someone who he thinks might understand his feelings. If the counselor refuses to compassionately understand the person's feelings or dismisses them as the result of failure to keep the commandments, insufficient faith, working too hard, and so on, then the counselor may lose his opportunity to help.

The depressed person needs to know that he is accepted. This can be a challenge for the counselor, since depressed people are often critical and demanding of themselves as well as their family, friends, and those trying to help them. As a counselor, when you recognize this symptom of depression, you will typically avoid the tendency to feel hurt by the rejection or criticism of the depressed person.

The troubled person can be helped by learning about the symptoms of depression discussed in this chapter. In many cases it is helpful to let the person know that he is experiencing a condition with certain predictable symptoms. This will help reduce the pressure he tends to put on himself. Many people, especially those with strong religious commitment, feel that emotional problems are strictly the result of deficient will or determination. This attitude is a part of their guilt feelings and actually stands in the way of easing their burdens. Recognizing that depression has predictable symptoms, the person may be able to examine some of his unrealistic expectations that may be a part of the depression.

A cardinal rule in the treatment of depression is to provide structure in the person's life. Those who are depressed tend to pull back from the world to avoid being reminded of their failures and inadequacies. By avoiding or denying their problems, they actually make them worse. By providing structure, a counselor helps the person function in the real world and also helps him become distracted from his obsessive feelings. Structure can be provided in a number of ways. Sensitive neighbors may be encouraged to develop recreation programs, to share hobbies, to set luncheon dates, or to provide outings. Part-time or full-time work, as well as volunteer activity, can provide structure. The counselor might pre-scribe a night of the week for the person and his or her spouse to go out together. And regular walking, jogging, or other exercise programs can be very helpful. It must be pointed out, however, that structured activity is usually the last thing the depressed person wants, and consequently he will require considerable encouragement and direction.

Since the depressed person feels such despair, it is impor-tant that he be offered a sense of hope from those who are trying to help. The counselor can provide hope by becoming quite active in the person's life. One of the symptoms of de-pression is difficulty in making decisions and seeing the world clearly. Anxiety, which usually accompanies depres-sion, has a very constricting quality. It produces a sort of emotional tunnel vision, making it difficult for him to see solutions to his problems. The anxious person can benefit from someone who can see further down the road. The kind of support and hope he requires does not come from patting him on the back, telling him things are not as bad as he thinks, or helping him count his blessings. The depressed person is likely to respond, "I have that many blessings and still I'm depressed; I'm a worse person than I thought—I'm ungrateful!" The support you should give is to help him see that you understand his feelings and that there are solutions to many of his problems, but that he is having trouble seeing them. He also needs to know that other people have felt as he feels and still have been able to survive (and even like them-selves). He can recognize that depression distorts his under-standing of reality—something the counselor can help him straighten out.

Generally, depressed people should be with others as much as possible. Long periods alone contribute to with-drawal and self-criticism. Isolated people tend to become self-centered and do not benefit from the give-and-take of social interaction. If they are living alone and depression is a serious concern, some attempt could be made to change their living arrangements so these needs might be met.

An Approach to Counseling

After many years of research, Dr. Aaron T. Beck has developed a treatment system that is becoming increasingly successful. Some of his principles can be used by the lay counselor to treat mild to moderate depressions. Dr. Beck has observed that three major belief patterns are part of most depressions. The first has to do with the person's negative views of himself. He believes himself to be inadequate or defective in some way and tends to attribute his failure and despair to this moral, psychological, or physical defect. Second, he views his present experience in a negative way. He feels that the world expects too much of him and that too many obstacles block his progress. The third belief is a negative view of the future. He is convinced that his current problems and suffering will continue indefinitely. He expects frustration and difficulties and is convinced he will fail at any task he tries. Generally speaking, all of these beliefs give the person the general feeling of hopelessness that is so typical of depression.

In evaluating the thinking of the depressed person, the counselor will typically find false assumptions that lead to depression and sadness. Some of these that have been discussed by Beck[3] include the following: (1) to be happy, I have to be successful at whatever I undertake; (2) to be happy, I must be accepted by all people at all times; (3) if I make a mistake, it means that I am a failure; (4) I can't live without my spouse; (5) if someone disagrees with me, it means he doesn't like me; (6) my value as a person depends on what others think of me. Some other false assumptions are these: (1) if I'm spiritual, bad things will not happen to me; (2) I should be able to make anyone love me; (3) good parents always love their children and never become angry with them; (4) good people are never angry and never have negative feelings.

Most depression is based on such false assumptions. These assumptions lead to false conclusions and automatic negative thoughts, which lead to catastrophic conclusions.

For example, a person may have this false assumption: If I am a loving person (suffer for others, do everything that's expected of me, always seem happy and pleasant), bad things (divorce, financial problems, disobedient children) won't happen to me. If so, he might conclude, It's my fault when bad things happen because I'm not loving and good enough. Such a conclusion then leads to automatic negative thoughts, which Beck says are a major cause of depression. Examples of such thoughts are (1) I caused my children to disobey; (2) I ruined my children's lives by getting a divorce; (3) I'm too selfish; (4) I never have good times; (5) I caused my spouse to have problems. Such thoughts may lead to such catastrophic conclusions as (1) my spouse will probably divorce me; (2) people will see what I'm like and fire me from my job; (3) I have disappointed God, so he will abandon me; (4) if I fail at something as basic as loving, I might as well be dead; (5) my children will fail and I will be responsible. Not surprisingly, such conclusions drive the person into despair.

The counselor can help the depressed person by identifying his false assumptions. However, as strange as it may seem, such beliefs are often near and dear to the person who has them. Even though his beliefs are irrational, the person judges his worth on how well he follows his beliefs. Simply calling the error to his attention will not be enough. The counselor will need to help him recognize the many times he thinks these self-defeating thoughts that lead to depression. Helping him do this must be done carefully and with sensitivity, or he may become defensive and angry.

The following list of assumptions and counseling strategies may help you counsel the depressed.[4]

False assumption: Failures are important, but successes are not.

Counseling strategy: Encourage the person to keep a written record of his successes and to talk with others to become aware of successes he has forgotten or overlooked.

Being willing to do something about depression is one success.

False assumption: I am totally responsible for the problems of other people.

Counseling strategy: Help the person recognize that many of the problems of others are out of his control. Other people have their own agency and make their own decisions, and they are ultimately responsible for their own problems and happiness. Only the Savior himself was able to bear the burdens of the whole world.

False assumption: I am the center of everyone's attention, especially when I make a mistake.

Counseling strategy: Help the person think of times when he really would be the center of attention and times when he would not. Help him distinguish between the two. Other people are probably paying less attention to him than he thinks. For example, few people would notice or even care if his shirt had a spot on it.

False assumption: The worst thing that could happen will happen.

Counseling strategy: Help the person understand how slim the chances are that the worst will always happen. You can do this by helping him remember that the worst has not usually happened in the past. For example, just because the person made a mistake at work does not mean he will automatically be fired.

Suicide

Anytime a person is depressed, and particularly if his feelings are severe, there is a strong possibility he has suicidal thoughts or intentions. The person will often drop clues about such feelings by making such comments as "I won't have to worry about Christmas next year," "I just can't stand it any longer," or "I can't face another day." He may give away prized possessions or develop unusual concerns about having a will drawn up. When a counselor knows that a person is depressed, especially if he sees some of the clues, he should directly question the person about suicidal feelings. Many depressed people, however, will try to hide these feelings because of the moral concerns associated with suicide. This should be taken into account, and the person should be helped to honestly evaluate his feelings. Any person who is clearly a suicidal risk should be referred immediately for professional help and possible hospitalization.

Most depressed people have suicidal thoughts from time to time even though they do not believe they would ever really commit suicide. *However, every statement of suicidal intent should be taken seriously. One should never assume that the person doesn't mean what he says.* If you are counseling someone with suicidal thoughts, the following strategies are important:[5] (1) Assure your availability. Let the person know where you can be reached if he is feeling despondent. (2) Counsel the person much more frequently than usual. You may want to require him to call you regularly. (3) Contact the person immediately if he cancels or fails to keep an appointment. (4) Get help from the person's family and friends, especially those who are sensitive and could help provide structure. (5) Make sure the person is not left alone for long periods of time. He may need to stay with a friend or enter the hospital. (6) If the person is being treated with medication, it is vital that the dosage be carefully monitored and that some responsible person dispense the medication, particularly if large quantities are available. (7) Appeal to the person's religious beliefs and family obligations to reduce the possibility of suicide. (8) Don't give empty reassurance. Saying something like, "Things aren't that bad; everyone feels blue once in a while," will likely alienate the person and make him feel you are not on his side.

Getting Help

Never underestimate the many resources available to help you. Professional mental health practitioners can be

consulted. Churches, families, and schools have been helping people for years.

Families can be made aware of the person's symptoms
and help him change his interpretation of his problems.
They can become more aware of his needs and become more
tolerant of his problems.

The Church has many resources, and Relief Society and
priesthood leaders can be very helpful. Professional help is
available from LDS Social Services.

Schools often have counseling programs, and they can
also provide opportunities for people to develop hobbies and
skills that promote self-esteem and decreased feelings of
helplessness.

All of these resources might be used to help the person
who is depressed. In addition, you should use your creativity
to come up with other resources that might be helpful but
have not yet been tapped.

NOTES

1. Aaron T. Beck, John A. Rush, Brian F. Shaw, Gary Emery, *Cognitive Therapy of Depression* (New York: Guilford Press, 1979).

2. Psychosis is a severe psychological disorder involving loss of contact with reality and gross personality distortion. Hospitalization is ordinarily required.

3. Aaron T. Beck, *Cognitive Therapy and the Emotional Disorders* (New York: International Universities Press, 1976), pp. 255-56.

4. Beck, et al, *Cognitive Therapy of Depression*, p. 261.

5. See Joan S. Zaro, Roland Barach, Deborah J. Nedelman, Irwin S. Dreiblatt, *A Guide for Beginning Psychotherapists* (Cambridge, England: Cambridge University Press, 1977).

ABOUT THE AUTHOR

Dr. David G. Weight, associate professor of psychology at Brigham Young University, received his bachelor's and master's degrees from that institution and his Ph.D. from the University of Washington. A highly respected clinical psychologist, Dr. Weight has had broad experience in therapeutic work in Washington and Utah. He is a consultant to Utah Valley Hospital Mental Health Services and a large Utah school district. He supervises a department of the BYU Comprehensive Clinic. Professor Weight has written a number of professional articles.

In the Church, Dr. Weight has served as a missionary, bishop, high councilor, and a Young Men's president.

He and his wife, Shauna, are the parents of five children.

Steps in Helping the Depressed

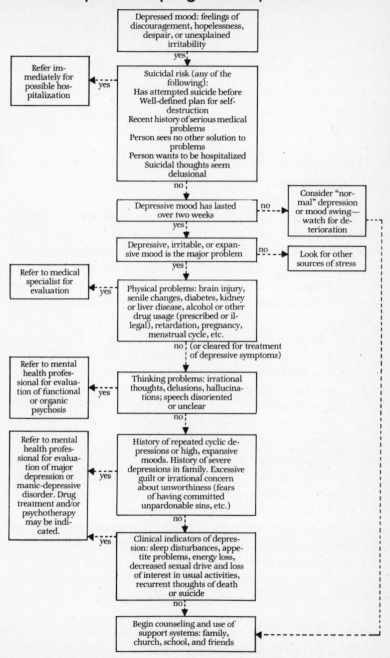

Depressed mood: feelings of discouragement, hopelessness, despair, or unexplained irritability

yes↓

Refer immediately for possible hospitalization ←--- yes --- Suicidal risk (any of the following):
Has attempted suicide before
Well-defined plan for self-destruction
Recent history of serious medical problems
Person sees no other solution to problems
Person wants to be hospitalized
Suicidal thoughts seem delusional

no↓

Depressive mood has lasted over two weeks --- no --→ Consider "normal" depression or mood swing—watch for deterioration

yes↓

Depressive, irritable, or expansive mood is the major problem --- no --→ Look for other sources of stress

yes↓

Refer to medical specialist for evaluation ←--- yes --- Physical problems: brain injury, senile changes, diabetes, kidney or liver disease, alcohol or other drug usage (prescribed or illegal), retardation, pregnancy, menstrual cycle, etc.

no (or cleared for treatment of depressive symptoms)↓

Refer to mental health professional for evaluation of functional or organic psychosis ←--- yes --- Thinking problems: irrational thoughts, delusions, hallucinations; speech disoriented or unclear

no↓

Refer to mental health professional for evaluation of major depression or manic-depressive disorder. Drug treatment and/or psychotherapy may be indicated. ←--- yes --- History of repeated cyclic depressions or high, expansive moods. History of severe depressions in family. Excessive guilt or irrational concern about unworthiness (fears of having committed unpardonable sins, etc.)

no↓

←--- yes --- Clinical indicators of depression: sleep disturbances, appetite problems, energy loss, decreased sexual drive and loss of interest in usual activities, recurrent thoughts of death or suicide

no↓

Begin counseling and use of support systems: family, church, school, and friends

5

Stress

Val R. Christensen

Nearly every Church leader has counseled someone with emotional or psychological conflict, commonly known as stress. Such a person may display a great amount of hostility, frustration, or anger. He may grieve from the loss of a loved one. Or, he may simply be overworked or burdened with heavy responsibilities. In most cases, he is not functioning effectively or enjoying a happy, well-balanced life.

The following situations often contribute to stress:

1. Not having enough time to accomplish everything.
2. Excessive guilt from unrepented sin.
3. Uncertainty about goals.
4. Dissatisfaction with employment.
5. Anxiety about a new Church calling.
6. Disagreement with a spouse or child.
7. Difficulty relating to neighbors or friends.
8. Disappointment with a child who has been involved in a moral transgression.
9. Difficulty showing love for in-laws.
10. Discouragement and hurt because a spouse has been unfaithful or has a serious alcohol problem.
11. Depression over having been fired from a job.
12. Disappointment in a family member who is not active in the Church.

What Is Stress?

Stress is the strong feeling of uncertainty one might have when he considers something important. Imagine that you

are walking down a trail in Yellowstone Park. It is a beautiful, tranquil day. Wild flowers are in bloom and chipmunks
scurry across the trail. Suddenly ahead of you appears a huge
grizzly bear. Your mind immediately directs the autonomic
nervous system and the endocrine glands to activate. This
speeds up the cardiovascular functions and slows down the
gastrointestinal operations, giving the body strength to
"fight or take flight." You suddenly have great strength to run
swiftly down the trail to safety.

The same kind of physical reaction can occur when you
have a fight with a family member or give a talk in sacrament meeting. Arguing with the boss about a difficult problem or confronting your teenager when he arrives home in
the early hours of the morning may have a similar effect. The
body responds in the same way, no matter what the stressful
situation.

Stress is not always bad. In fact, it is often helpful. It may
help you run from a bear or motivate you to solve family
problems. The harm comes as you dwell on the stressful
situation and worry that the problem will recur. For example, you pitch your tent at night in an enclosed camping
area and crawl into your sleeping bag but continue to fret
that a bear may attack you in your sleep. If you allow stress to
linger too long, it becomes *distress* or *strain*.

Distress is stress out of control. Once stress is allowed,
often by your own inaction, to cross the fine line into distress,
it no longer helps you handle pressure from without, but it
begins to weaken your body and to increase the likelihood of
disease and emotional upheaval. The amount of distress a
person can handle depends upon a number of factors, such
as heredity, personality, habits, past accidents, illnesses, and
physical well-being. Some stress may help us function at our
peak. But if pressures continue for long periods of time, serious problems can develop, including physical and emotional
illness.

Signs of Stress
Counselors should be sensitive to behavior that indicates

harmful levels of stress. Dr. John Adams lists the most common symptoms:[1]

1. *Disregard for low or high priority tasks.* A wife refuses to get up in the morning. A student neglects studying. A leader stops going to meetings or fails to follow through on assignments. A teacher fails to prepare a lesson or to show up for class. When a person abandons his efforts to be productive, he may have crossed that dangerous line to distress.

2. *Reduced time given to a task.* A child suddenly refuses to take enough time for important assignments such as cleaning his room or mowing the lawn. A father reduces his time spent with his family. A wife does not give adequate attention to homemaking. Sudden changes such as these may be attributed to outside pressures.

3. *Shifting responsibility.* One child tries to shift responsibilities to another child. A Relief Society president delegates more than is reasonable. A scoutmaster asks other members of the ward to take on his responsibilities. Such shifts may be related to stress.

4. *Blocking out new information.* A Sunday School president reacts negatively when suggestions are made for improving teaching in the ward. A father becomes abusive when his wife offers advice to help improve his relationship with their children. Such reactions often reflect a breakdown of resistance due to pressures at home or work.

5. *Superficial involvement or appearing to give up.* A ward officer tells the bishop he does not want to continue in his calling because it is too overwhelming. A student fails in school because of problems at home. A spouse dissolves a marriage because the effort needed to improve the relationship seems too great. People who abandon a project or relationship often do so as a way of dealing with stress.

6. *Negative attitude or cynicism about friends or family.* A person who constantly expresses negative feelings about others often does so because of stress. If people who are generally positive suddenly become negative, they may be reacting to pressures from work or family.

7. *Impersonal or detached behavior.* Occasionally a per-

son under stress is not able or willing to carry on a friendly conversation or cannot concentrate for long periods of time. He may appear cold, aloof, and uncaring.

8. *Going strictly by the book.* Sometimes a person becomes so strict and inflexible that others cannot work with them. Teachers, leaders, or parents who insist that every rule be followed without alteration cause themselves and others a great amount of stress. Such inflexibility may be a result of prolonged pressure and stress.

9. *Inappropriate humor.* Sometimes a person laughs at tragedy or at incidents that are not generally considered funny, or he tries to be funny when the situation does not call for it. This may be a reaction to stress.

10. *Absenteeism.* A person who begins to miss meetings or fails to arrive home at his usual time may be reacting to outside pressures. Such pressures may cause a reduced interest in important activities.

There are other signs of stress. People under stress are often overexcited, worry a great deal, feel insecure, cannot sleep at night, or are easily confused and forgetful. Physical symptoms include upset stomach, pounding heart, profuse sweating, moist hands, lightheadedness, fainting episodes, cold chills, and flushed face. Other possible symptoms are trembling fingers or hands, inability to sit or stand still, severe headaches, tense muscles, stammering, or a stiff neck.

Once a counselor recognizes the symptoms of stress, he should begin to examine the three dimensions of the person's life that affect stress. These dimensions are physical, interpersonal, and spiritual.

The Physical Dimension

The physical dimension includes exercise and nutrition. Many Church members do not pay adequate attention to these areas. In a world where only a few jobs require strenuous physical activity, most people are terribly out of shape. They ride cars and buses rather than walk, and they use elevators instead of stairs. Once a person has the endorsement of a physician, he should begin a regular exercise program to build body strength. Then he should be able to maintain good physical condition with three or four thirty-minute exercise sessions each week. People on a regular exercise program tend to handle stress more effectively.

Nutrition also makes a difference in how people handle stress. People should be encouraged to eat a balanced diet and maintain proper weight. We often rely on convenience foods that are unnecessarily high in calories, salt, and additives. A good eating plan based on a balanced diet of cereals and grains, vegetables, fruits, dairy products and meats is important in withstanding stress. A good stress-fighting diet minimizes the use of sugar, salt, saturated fats, artificial additives, alcohol, tobacco, and caffeine. When counseling someone suffering from stress, the counselor should ask about his physical activity and eating habits and suggest possible changes, in consultation with competent medical and nutritional professionals.

The Interpersonal Dimension

An important factor in coping with stress is developing a support network of people to turn to for help. Often a person is not able to eliminate pressure but can receive love and concern from family and friends. Often those who are unable to solve their problems are isolated from others who might be of help. An effective counselor will help the troubled person stay close to such people. Bishops, quorum leaders, home teachers, and visiting teachers can often do much to help those under stress. For some problems, especially marriage difficulties, people outside of the family can sometimes provide more effective and objective assistance than can family members. It is important to ask a distressed person who he knows that might be able to help him.

People who have many friends and associates often work through problems more rapidly than do those who feel alone or alienated. Those who have close relationships with only one or two people limit themselves in effectively coping with stress. For this reason, counselors should encourage people to develop a broad range of friends and associates.

The Spiritual Dimension

Spirituality is feeling close to God. Those who do not feel God's influence are often lonely and troubled. Such spiritual isolation is usually a result of sin. Those who commit adultery, who fail to pay tithing, or who do not regularly attend church often feel stress.

Someone who has been an active member of the Church but who begins to fall away will probably alienate himself not only from God but also from Church leaders, family members, and friends. Consequently, he may have a negative attitude toward Church leaders or doctrine. Likewise, he may cause arguments and other problems at home.

For a person to work through such problems and to learn to be obedient to gospel principles may take time, but confessing and forsaking transgressions can greatly reduce stress. Helping a person return to God may be the most important thing a counselor can do.

Sometimes a counselor makes the mistake of considering only one dimension of a person's life. The counselor may advise him to pray, read the scriptures, or attend church. But it is most effective to explore all three dimensions carefully to understand the breadth of the problem. To encourage someone to read the scriptures or to pray may not entirely solve the problem. Likewise, to suggest exercise as a way to reduce stress may not remove the loneliness, confusion, and alienation from friends or from a good relationship with our Father in Heaven. All three dimensions are important.

Coping with Stress

In addition to helping someone analyze the three dimensions of his life, the counselor can use other principles:

1. *Talk out troubles.* People should be encouraged to talk about their problems with someone they like and respect. Most people just need to talk through their problems. They don't need advice on how to solve them, but merely need a listening ear. It helps to share worries with someone else. This is not admitting defeat; it is admitting that one knows when to ask for help.

2. *Learn to accept what can't be changed.* Some problems are beyond control and can't be solved. In such instances, the person should be encouraged to accept the situation until change is possible. Such acceptance in itself may reduce the pressure.

3. *Plan daily activities.* Many people under stress try to accomplish too much at once. People who are able to plan their activities tend to work through problems more effectively. Helping people plan their activities so that every aspect of their lives does not seem hurried can greatly reduce their stress.

4. *Avoid loneliness.* People should be encouraged to reach out to others. If they will take the initiative to make friends, they will have someone to turn to during difficult times.

5. *Deal with the cause.* If the person's tension comes from a deteriorating relationship, he should be encouraged to talk out his differences with the other person involved. The longer a broken relationship continues, the more stressful it becomes. If stress comes from an important unfinished task, the person should be urged to change his priorities to accomplish the task.

6. *Plan for change.* Many people experience stress because they put too many activities into their lives at the same time. Moving into a new house, buying a new car, having a new child, going away to school, taking a new job, and accepting a calling in the Church are all major changes in a person's life. If possible, one should spread such changes out over a period of time. A person approaching retirement might prepare by gradually working fewer hours over two or three years. A person who has a divorce should wait awhile before seeking new employment, moving, or remarrying. Spacing important events allows a person to adjust to them without undue stress.

7. *Develop a positive and patient disposition.* Nothing is gained by worry. Rather than fretting about a problem, one should take steps to solve it. Those who have a history of distress tend to look at life negatively. Positive attitudes help

solve problems and even fight disease, while negative ones intensify problems or illness.

8. *Balance work with play.* It is important for people to have hobbies and other recreation. It is especially important to include family and friends in recreational activities. Planning unstructured vacations or spontaneous outings reduces pressure and provides renewal. People should loaf a little—go to movies, read books, and simply get away from it all.

9. *Don't be afraid to compromise when disagreements do not involve moral issues.* People should be encouraged to give in once in a while. There are usually alternatives to fighting or sulking. Sometimes it is important to honor the other person's preference. Inflexible people often feel a considerable amount of stress.

10. *Nurture inner peace.* Inner peace comes from obedience to the commandments. It is also a by-product of a purposeful life. People should be encouraged to live righteously and to do things that develop confidence and a sense of accomplishment.

11. *Have devotional time every day.* Most people work too long and hard without taking time out to meditate, read the scriptures, and pray. One should take at least two short devotional periods each day to reduce pressure and return to a more relaxed state.

12. *Rise above defeats.* Often, stress occurs when a person feels defeated or unworthy. It is important to help people understand that the depressing thought of being a failure can often be eliminated by recalling past achievements and successes. Looking to the future by setting new goals can also help reduce the effects of defeat.

13. *Accept imperfection.* Some people are their own worst enemies—they expect too much of themselves. Of course, we should aim for perfection, but we should not be depressed or frustrated if we do not always achieve it. Failure is part of being mortal, and perfection is achieved one step at a time. (See D&C 93:11-20.)

14. *Concentrate on enriching yourself.* Many people under

stress have not expanded their lives beyond family or church activities. People should be encouraged to engage in a variety of activities to help build confidence and relationships. People whose lives are varied, active, and productive are able to adjust to sudden changes without undue stress. Homemakers especially should do something enjoyable every day. A homemaker might paint a picture, write a story, send a note to a friend, decorate a room, or sew some new clothes.

15. *Avoid self-pity.* People should be encouraged to do something for others. They should reach out to someone who needs help and concentrate their concern on another person's problems rather than always focusing on their own. People under stress often concentrate too much on themselves and their own problems.

Conclusion

It is important for people to understand the impact that stress can have on their lives. Some stress is necessary. But when worry, jealousy, anger, or sorrow become too much for one to bear, he may need help. Counselors can help a person under stress to analyze the three dimensions of his life—physical, interpersonal, and spiritual—and then suggest ways to reduce stress.

NOTE

1. John D. Adams, *Understanding and Managing Stress: A Book of Readings* and *A Workbook in Changing Life Styles* (San Diego: University Associates, 1980).

SUGGESTED READINGS

John D. Adams, *Understanding and Managing Stress: A Book of Readings* (San Diego: University Associates, 1980).

—————, *Understanding and Managing Stress: A Workbook in Changing Life Styles* (San Diego: University Associates, 1980).

Ramona Adams, Herbert Otto, and Au-Deane Cowley, *Letting Go: Uncomplicating Your Life* (New York: MacMillan Publishing Co., 1980).

Hans Selye, *Stress Without Distress* (New York: J.B. Lippincott, 1974).

ABOUT THE AUTHOR

Dr. Val R. Christensen, vice president of student affairs at Utah State University, received his bachelor's and master's degrees from Utah State University and his Ph.D.

from Michigan State University in higher education administration. Well known in northern Utah as a lecturer on LDS topics, Dr. Christensen has years of teaching and administrative experience at the high school and college levels. He has published several articles in the *Ensign* and in a number of professional publications.

In the Church, Dr. Christensen is presently president of the Logan Utah East Stake. Previous callings include counselor in a USU campus stake presidency, bishop, bishop's counselor, stake mission president, and Young Men's president.

He and his wife, Ruth Ann, are the parents of five children.

6

Loneliness
Cathleen Sue Croxton

Man was not created to be alone, yet loneliness afflicts all—young and old, bond and free, rich and poor, healthy and sick, righteous and wicked. It was the lot of Joseph of old, of Joseph Smith, of Job, and even Christ to feel alone, forsaken, and abandoned for a time so that they might fill the measure of their creation. This chapter will explain what loneliness is and what its probable causes are. It will also discuss how counselors and friends can best help the lonely.

What Is Loneliness?

Loneliness is being without the presence or support of those who are congenial to one's interests, temperament, viewpoint, or way of life. It is to be without those who share one's situation. It is to be empty, to be void of some influence that one would like to have. For some, loneliness means discomfort; for others, despair. For some it is trial; for others, temptation.

The fall of Adam made possible this mortal probation, and we are free to do what is right or to sin. But we all sin, and sin promotes loneliness in several ways. First, when we sin, we remove ourselves from the Spirit of God. Since God is the source of the deepest love and companionship available to us, this separation creates great loneliness and misery. Second, sin can create gulfs between family members or friends. These gulfs cause loneliness for the sinner and for

those who love him. Third, because of our weaknesses, we
are given experiences to strengthen us and confirm our loyalty to God. This is the purpose of our mortal probation. In
many instances, loneliness is the testing ground where faithfulness is tried and strengthened.

Adam's fall also brought death, and all of us have experienced or will yet experience the death of a loved one. Regardless of the courage of those who meet this challenge, they are
still without that person for the rest of their lives.

The suffering associated with loneliness resulting from
sin and death is meant to turn our hearts to God for comfort
and peace. We are taught by Lehi in 2 Nephi 2 that there
must be opposition in all things. If we do not know suffering,
we can never know joy. Suffering, therefore, is necessary so
that we might know a fullness of joy as does God. Regardless
of the cause of the suffering, it can be a blessing. It can turn
us to God, and it gives us experience to prepare us to help and
to be helped. It refines, teaches, strengthens, and sanctifies.

Preparing to Counsel the Lonely

In cultivating our desire and our ability to serve, we must
begin with our own hearts. Are we willing and able to be
charitable? Are we willing and able to discover what charity
might demand in various situations? What does charity
mean in connection with counseling the lonely? The definition of charity gives some excellent suggestions that might be
used in counseling the lonely: "And charity suffereth long,
and is kind, and envieth not, and is not puffed up, seeketh
not her own, is not easily provoked, thinketh no evil, and rejoiceth not in iniquity but rejoiceth in the truth, beareth all
things, believeth all things, hopeth all things, endureth all
things." (Moroni 7:45.)

Your kindness and consideration may be the greatest gift
you could give to a lonely person. By recognizing that his feelings are real and normal, you can help him create meaningful relationships by deepening and developing the one you
have with him.

Sometimes a lonely person becomes uncharitable, accusatory, and bitter about his circumstances. This might provoke uncharitable responses in you. If so, you would not be able to help him. For example, a lonely mother might say, "My son makes me sick. All his life I served him, cleaned up after him, cooked for him. I was the best mother he could have asked for. And now that I'm old and can't get out to see him, do you think he comes to see me? Can you blame me for hating him?" If you were to accept her attitude and by your response support her feelings, you would be helping her carry enmity in her heart rather than forgiveness and peace. By helping her maintain hatred, you would be accepting her sin by sinning with her.

It is possible to concoct feelings such as loneliness and to use these feelings to blame and accuse others. Often these accusatory feelings represent some personal refusal to be obedient to the commandments, to love God, neighbor, and self. A person concocting such feelings might say, "How can I love my son? Look at how he neglects and abuses me. Obviously *I* am not responsible for not loving him. It's *his* fault. *He* is responsible for my not keeping the commandments; my suffering and loneliness are proof. If he treated me in a way that made him lovable, I could love him, but my loneliness is proof that he is definitely not lovable."

Such feelings might be described as pseudo-loneliness, for while the person feels empty and angry, her attitudes are not purifying, but are a refusal to be true to what is right. She concocts her feelings as evidence or justification. The feelings are real but false.

The refusal to accept responsibility for one's own failure to be charitable often provokes the counselor to refute or to accept the person's insistence that she is not responsible for her suffering. Both reactions will only encourage the person's negative feelings. The counselor should not accept provocation no matter what form it takes. He should help turn the lonely person's hostile heart to the gospel. In the above example, the woman's son may be wrong in not visiting her, but she can seek ways, in charity, of not being part of the problem. Her own charity will restore her personal peace.

She may still be lonely, but instead of hating her son, she will feel sorrow for him.

When our thoughts concerning the lonely are loving, we can see the lonely as a blessing to our lives, for they bring us the opportunity to serve them and to be served by them. But if we view the lonely in a negative way, we will not be able to serve them. We should avoid thoughts like these: "Why can't this person take care of his own problems? He demands so much of my time and energy, and I don't have it to give. I feel like a heel if I don't try to help and I feel as if he takes advantage of me if I do." Such thoughts produce a seeming dilemma in which both alternatives are unattractive. If we look deeply into our hearts, though, we will always find that another alternative exists—charity.

Helping the Lonely

Here are some ways to charitably help the lonely.

Help the lonely person discover the source of his loneliness. Together, explore the lonely person's situation. It may be helpful to ask him to spend a certain amount of time each day pondering the meaning of his loneliness until he has arrived at an honest understanding of his problem. This may promote introspection that reveals the true source of the problem, a source that might otherwise go unrecognized or misunderstood. Suppose the friend you are counseling lives in an area where she has few friends her own age. You recommend that she move to an area where she will be closer to people her own age, but she refuses. She complains that she has lived where she is for many years and that a move would be too difficult for her mentally and physically. This may be true, but she may simply be afraid to move. She may not feel that she will be accepted in a new place by new people. Unless she takes time to understand her feelings, she may never realize what her real fear is and be able to improve her circumstances.

Sometimes a person is lonely because he needs to repent but is too busy covering his tracks to yield to the truth. By setting aside time to consider his situation, he may slow down

long enough to consider the possibility that he is his own
source of loneliness and can therefore be his own source of
happiness. By encouraging him to pray and study, you can
help him understand the real problem.

Many people do not want to know the source of their
problems, although they say they do. They do not want to
know because they do not want to change. You may sometime have heard a conversation like this one:

Betty:	Sandy, I feel crummy.
Sandy:	What's wrong?
Betty:	I'm so lonely. I want to get out and meet people.
Sandy:	Me too. Why don't you come with me to the party we've been invited to?
Betty:	No, I don't think I want to go.
Sandy:	Why not?
Betty:	Because if I went, no one would pay any attention to me. I'd be just as lonely there as I am here.
Sandy:	Would you pay attention to the people at the party?
Betty:	Not really. I figure if they wanted to get to know me, they would make the effort.

What would happen if Sandy persuaded Betty to go to the
party but Betty's attitude stayed the same? Betty would stand
defiantly or martyr-like alone against the wall, her demeanor
defying anyone to try to change her mind about the cold,
cruel world. Of course no one would try to get to know her.
Outwardly she might appear to have changed because she
went to the party, but her real goal of accusing the world
would not have changed at all. Only her way of doing so
would be different. Betty would still be in the business of
being alone, and until she decides to see the world less accusingly, you could do little to help her. For instance, you might
say, "Betty, if you would change your attitude, you would be
so much happier." But she would reply, "I'm not going to
accept responsibility for everyone else's insensitivity. My attitude might be bad, but whose wouldn't be if they faced rejection like I do?"

If you were to drop by for a visit, how would Betty accept
it? She might see it as a pity visit: "He just feels sorry for me.

He thinks I'm a social misfit or something." Of course, Betty might not respond in this way. In fact, your visit might be the very thing she needs. But until she is willing to give up her accusing attitude and see your visit for what it is, her problems won't be solved. When people truly want to change their situations or perspectives, they will seek to understand the source of their problems. Then you can really work together.

You may be able to understand some things about the lonely person and his situation that he does not. For example, a man we'll call Mark almost completely neglects his personal hygiene. Because of his upbringing, he is totally unaware of the problem. Mark is distressed because no one will befriend him. Although such a situation is less subtle than many you might face, being tactfully honest about a person's causes of loneliness could benefit him greatly.

Help the lonely person get involved in constructive activity. Become aware of the opportunities in your area for service to individuals, families, schools, churches, and the community that you could recommend to the lonely. Many people have lost themselves in service only to discover that the only thing they have really lost is their loneliness. Service helps relieve the mind and heart of suffering.

Whenever possible, recommend service that is related to the person's needs. Avoid service that will cause further discomfort. For instance, it may help a childless couple to fellowship another childless couple into Church activity.

If necessary, remind the lonely person that his service might not result in the fulfillment of a specific desire, such as finding a spouse. Help him to render service for its own sake, not for the rewards it might bring.

When a person is seeking a particular type of relationship, help him focus on what he needs to do to develop it. For example, suppose a man who is widowed with children came to you and told you that he needs to find a wife. He is lonely for companionship and at the same time wants his children to enjoy a mother again. But he is financially irresponsible and is deep in debt, which frightens his marriage prospects away. He needs to learn the principles of money management. While you might not feel qualified to teach him those principles, you might be able to point out the problem and find someone else to teach him.

Help the person understand that when the Lord has laid a course for him it is important that he submit to that course. You might use Job as an example to teach this concept. Job suffered severe loneliness. He was forsaken by family, friends, and associates. Even though he was sorely afflicted, he would not curse God. He remained faithful and submissive to the Lord. His submission did not change because he was miserable, nor did his misery change because he wished it to. It did not change until he proved himself faithful.

When you can see that a person has done all he can to alleviate his suffering, it might help to explore the idea that his suffering is necessary. So often we hear people say, "Boy, have I been tried this week!" or "The Lord must really be preparing me for something great to put me through all this." The self-congratulatory attitude that sparks such statements is not what is meant by necessary suffering. What is being suggested is comfort for those who can learn and grow from their trials.

Help the person understand that his loneliness does not necessarily mean that his life is unacceptable before God. Again, Job is an excellent example. Several of Job's closest friends rebuked him in the name of God's justice for sins that he had not committed. They eventually reaped the vengeance of God while Job was blessed for his faithfulness.

If the lonely person thinks his loneliness is punishment for sin, discuss that possibility. If it appears that his loneliness is a natural consequence of wrongdoing, encourage him to repent. However, if he has an incorrect understanding of the consequences of sin, correct his misconceptions. For example, a woman who feels that her husband's death and her ensuing loneliness are a result of her failure to pay tithing needs better understanding of justice and of cause-and-effect relationships.

Encourage the lonely person to be willing to be loved. So much loneliness can be averted if we will let people into our lives and hearts. When we accept service, we are also serving. Encourage the lonely to reach out to family, friends, and Church members in times of both need and rejoicing.

Don't be afraid to contact others and invite them to befriend a lonely person. This is especially important when the person is elderly, restricted in activity, or confined to one place. After finding out the needs of the person, ask for help from those who might give it.

When the lonely person is living in or working in conditions that increase their loneliness, suggest a change in surroundings. The aged generally enjoy association with their peers just as do the middle-aged and the young. While a move or a change of employment may seem threatening, it may do much to revitalize a dull, dreary life. Friends and associates in the church and community can help make such changes less frightening and more feasible.

When the person has few or no hobbies or interests, try to arouse interest in one or several that would lead the person to self-fulfillment and association with others. There are many organizations, clubs, and community and church groups based on specific interests and activities that provide the opportunity for both a social climate and fulfilling activity.

Be consistent in your concern for the person's welfare. Such consistency may be the catalyst that sparks their willingness and confidence to overcome their obstacles.

In brief, perhaps the most important thing to remember is to help the lonely, in faith, imagine the ways out of their difficulties. Such a goal will help diminish hopelessness and increase activity.

ABOUT THE AUTHOR

Cathleen Sue Croxton, a homemaker, received her bachelor's degree in psychology and is a candidate for a master's degree in family sciences from Brigham Young University. She has counseled and taught courses in child development and family relations.

She has held a number of positions in the Church, including Relief Society counselor, Relief Society stake board member, and teacher for various teaching organizations.

She and her husband, Brent, and their child live in Dallas, Texas.

7

LOSS
W. Eugene Gibbons

> Now Abraham and Sarah were old and well stricken in age; and it
> ceased to be with Sarah after the manner of women. Therefore Sarah
> laughed within herself, saying, After I am waxed old shall I have
> pleasure, my Lord being old also? (Genesis 18:11-12.)

It is difficult to understand fully the depth and complexity of Sarah's feelings when she learned that her future was to be different than she had supposed. Since she was mortal, subject to the same trials and feelings we all face, we might suspect she had anguished greatly over her barren state. It is obvious that the bearing of Isaac was a great blessing to Sarah, and she may even have viewed her previous inability to have children as an invalidation of herself as a woman or a wife. As many women in the Church know, such a limitation is often viewed as a loss. There are many similarities between Sarah's experience and our experiences today.

We understand that this life is not intended to be without stress, pain, and difficulty, and loss is simply part of life. Unfortunately, many people are not prepared to accept the reality that loss and pain are unavoidable and that ultimately they can be sources of growth.

What Is Loss?

There are five main categories of loss: (1) death; (2) loss of social role (through divorce, inability to bear children, single parenthood, etc.); (3) loss of employment; (4) loss of health or body function (through stroke, heart attack, hysterectomy, loss of limb, paralysis, mastectomy, etc.); (5) loss of self-esteem (from deciding not to go on a mission, from marrying outside the temple, from being an unwed mother, from lack of affluence, etc.).

Since loss is a universal experience, the problem for those who counsel is to understand how people perceive their loss, how they respond emotionally to it, and what they are doing about it. Dr. Elisabeth Kübler-Ross has identified the stages a person may pass through in one of the greatest losses, the death of a loved one. The steps are (1) denial (shock); (2) anger (emotion); (3) bargaining; (4) preparatory depression; and (5) acceptance (increased self-awareness and self-reliance).[1] My professional practice has taught me that even though death is only one form of loss, the stages described by Kübler-Ross may apply to all forms of loss. The question may not be whether people will pass through such stages, but rather where, why, when, and for how long they might become entangled in one of the stages. It is typical for people to experience these stages, and it would be a great disservice to those we seek to help if we automatically assume they are incapable of successfully dealing with loss simply because they manifest unusual behavior or other signs of stress. We must guard against any suggestion to those in mourning that they are unequal to the tasks before them or that they should not be called upon to bear such heavy burdens. Even though painful, loss can and ultimately must be understood and accepted as a challenge, an opportunity for growth, and a way to discover the purposes of life.

Responses to Loss

People face loss with varying degrees of emotional strength, intellectual ability, personal discipline, and with various philosophies of life. For example, complaints about loss do nothing to change that loss and must ultimately be given up. M. Scott Peck, in his book *The Road Less Traveled*, says, "Most do not fully see . . . that life is difficult. Instead, they moan more or less incessantly, noisily, or subtly, about the enormity of their problems, their burdens, and their difficulties as if life were generally easy, or as if life should be easy. They voice their belief, noisily or subtly, that their difficulty represents a unique kind of affliction that should not be and that has somehow been especially visited upon them, or else upon their families, even their species, and not upon others."[2]

The responses to our help from those who are dependent, irresponsible, impulsive, or critical may be quite different from the responses of those who look to the future with faith. Some people's only strength will be our own faith in their future. Other people will display astonishing courage in the face of great loss. A beautiful, young, Orem, Utah, teenager recently lost an all-out struggle with leukemia, but this young lady, who was courageous far beyond her years, became a symbol of hope to others. The world has been told of her zest for life, of her great faith in a kind, loving Heavenly Father, and of her determination to find purpose and meaning in her own suffering. Strength, courage, joy, and lasting unity grew out of her family's crisis and loss. The support provided by friends, religious leaders, and others, was accepted much more deeply by the leukemia victim because of her uncomplaining determination. Had she been a constant complainer or resentful of her lot, she might have spurned any help offered by others.

It is probable, then, that we who would help others will be seen quite differently by the different individuals we wish to help. Nevertheless, different people suffering from loss may have similar feelings, frustrations, and fears, so our role with them will need to be constant. Our concern for them and our acknowledgment of their unique personalities prepares us to help them.

Perhaps the most striking symptoms of loss are the troubled person's many emotional and physical problems. These may include hostility, anger, guilt, loneliness, feelings of rejection, self-pity, irritability, despair, helplessness, numbness, low self-esteem, loss of identity, sleeplessness, anxiety, fatigue, isolation, bewilderment, confusion, loss of appetite, shortness of breath, apprehension, alienation, depression, dependency, and a sense of unreality. Obviously, all people do not experience all of these symptoms, but most manifest various combinations of them.

Two rather universal emotions experienced by those in crisis are powerlessness and loss of control. Panic is often a result. Such emotions are usually associated with dependency on others, which can cause many other problems. Generally, a sense of personal control will not return until the afflicted person works to resolve his feelings, thus becoming an actor rather than a reactor.

Support

Our support is critical to helping the person resolve his feelings, and fundamental to that support is our belief that the grieving person *is* capable of doing so.

Perhaps the most important thing a counselor can do is to treat the troubled person as an individual. It is thoughtless, insensitive, and demeaning to treat a person as an object. We sometimes assume we know what a neighbor is going through simply because we have watched someone else struggle with a similar problem. But even members of the same family react differently to exactly the same loss. However, it is often difficult to know what another person is going through. Often a person experiencing loss will cling as long as possible to what he perceives as an "expected" behavior, and it may be some time before we can discern the depth of his feelings. Sometimes a person will present a facade, such as a "stiff upper lip," while experiencing overwhelming fears and stress.

Relating to the Troubled Person

Your success in helping someone who is suffering from loss will depend on the kind of relationship you have with him. Most people are very protective of what they say and how they disclose feelings. Their experiences may have taught them how unwise it is to spontaneously trust and confide in others. If the troubled person senses any insincerity, lack of interest, or emotional aloofness in you, he will probably deny his feelings and refuse to discuss his problems. He is already struggling and will not risk losing more to you through premature trust. Therefore, your first task is to develop the person's trust and confidence. Perhaps the quickest way to destroy these two essentials is to be too quick with false hope, easy answers, and insincere or hollow reassurances. The person suffering the loss will know in a moment that you are responding from your own discomfort and that your advice probably has little value. Your genuine concern, support, and encouragement is what is needed. Your relationship may not be established with a casual five-minute talk in the hall or with a fifteen-minute phone call.

It is not unusual for a person suffering from loss to be quite receptive to building new relationships, and if you are sensitive, empathic, and genuinely concerned, the person will be open to your help. Most of all, be yourself, be natural, be sincere. A spontaneous squeeze of the hand, an embrace, the unexpected phone call, and other gestures of concern and genuineness are invaluable.

As the relationship strengthens, it is not uncommon for the troubled person to depend on you more than he normally would. This should not be of particular concern to you. Just be careful not to encourage unnecessary dependency that moves someone away from, rather than toward, self-reliance. You will not complete your task as a counselor until the person is capable of making his own decisions and is independent of you.

Giving Reassurance

In the early stages of your counseling, it is important to help the troubled person identify and discuss his feelings and fears. He needs to be reassured that his experience and feelings are natural and that he has not suddenly lost his mind or turned from the Lord. But be careful not to deny that his feelings are real.

Most people are ashamed to admit feelings of anger or ambivalence, as they sense it communicates to others that they no longer have control over what is happening or what has happened to them. Anger and ambivalence are not necessarily signs of hopelessness, but are real feelings that you can acknowledge while offering hope that change can come.

Timing and Additional Resources

One of the troubled person's great assets is his concerned friends, neighbors, and family members, who can give tremendous emotional support. But in giving this support, we may spend so much time with the person that he has no time to be alone to ponder his loss. A person may need time to reflect, meditate, and understand what is happening to him. He will not have this time if he is always surrounded by well-meaning people who are constantly offering support and encouragement. On the other hand, many friends may have a tendency to abandon the person after a week or two. His greatest grief and pain often come after the immediate crisis, long after most of his friends have stopped visiting and checking on him. It takes time to deal with loss, and those who are helping someone troubled by loss need to understand this and be available for quite some time. A good counselor will help the person explore how he feels several weeks or months after his loss. These feelings will reveal his direction, his progress in finding answers to his problems.

Helping People Solve Problems

Perhaps the best way to help is to teach problem-solving skills. During a crisis, most people do not think things through in an organized or logical fashion. Many people feel overwhelmed by their circumstances, and logic has little relevance for them. It is important to help the person think clearly and act responsibly. As discussed earlier, it is also important to help him understand his feelings, but it will not help him to go on hour after hour bemoaning his situation and indulging himself in his feelings. Sometimes the person may be overwhelmed by irrational fears that need to be confronted. If carried too far, such behavior, if unchallenged, reinforces the person's hopelessness and helplessness. It confirms his feelings of loss of control and suggests that the answers to his problems can be found only outside of himself. This creates an unhealthy dependency and invalidates the person as a responsible, capable parent, mate, child, and human being.

After he has sorted out his feelings, the person suffering loss needs to set some realistic and appropriate goals to help him get on with his life. If he seems to have little information to help him make responsible decisions, you can help him find the information he needs. To gather data and to think of possible solutions and their consequences may be of great help to those who have suffered great loss. It will help prevent the impulsive, emotional behavior so often observed in those who are unable to cope with loss effectively. A friend and colleague, Dr. Dave Seamons, developed the worksheet at the end of this chapter to help people solve problems.

It is helpful to ask the person with a problem to define or describe it. Then, seek their ideas as to what solutions they can think of. Write these under "strategies." You might offer additional alternatives. It is fine to write down some wildly unrealistic solutions to help improve creative thinking and to add some humor to the process.

Do not be too quick to suggest that some choice be made from among the alternatives. It may be better to send the person home to ponder additional alternatives. The important thing about using this form is that it provides concrete possibilities to the person who feels overwhelmed.

Avoid imposing pat answers and solutions on the person. If he follows your suggestions and they work poorly, he need not assume responsibility for the failure, as it was not his idea. In addition, he may not try very hard to make the idea work since he did not help come up with the idea. The idea might be completely inappropriate for his situation, which he alone really understands. If your idea is successful, the person may come back for more help and eventually become dependent on you.

Even though the decision-making may take longer than if you were just to give quick suggestions, it is better to sit down and work through the issues with the person so that the alternatives are carefully evaluated before one is selected. The time spent fostering self-reliance in solving problems will increase the likelihood of the problem being solved.

Seeking Spiritual Direction

A person suffering from loss may find prayer of great help. However, if a person is blinded by denial, anger, or guilt, he may resist the very spiritual solace he could receive. It is wise to link logical decisions to spiritual guidance. Rarely is it appropriate to promote the idea that there are practical answers apart from prayerful ones. We wish to promote the notion that *prayer is practical*, though it does not stand alone. Prayer is an absolute necessity, but it is especially useful after the person has gathered information, pondered alternatives, and made some tentative decisions. Of course, prayer is helpful at any time.

In Conclusion

Most people can resolve their loss without suffering deep or longstanding emotional or psychological problems. However, when those who already have problems are also faced with loss, more serious complications can arise. Seriously depressed people who are potential suicides should be referred to professionals rather quickly. Angry, hostile, dependent people with low self-esteem may not be particularly dangerous, but they can resist your attempts to help by constant negative thoughts and feelings. They can take all your time and energy if you let them. In some cases, it may be well to refer them to professionals. If you continue to counsel them, you may need to structure your time in a manner that permits at least weekly visits. However, refuse to be on twenty-four-hour call. Plan your meetings in such a way that the people you help will learn to anticipate the occasion as their special opportunity to discuss feelings, problems, and potential solutions with you. They may not learn to discipline their emotions or to search themselves first for solu-

tions if they can call every night at 11:00 P.M.! Your suffering
friend will be angry if you permit and foster dependency because he knows this is not good; but he will also be angry if
you fail to meet his demands and needs. Thus, the only sure
way of helping such a person is to place the responsibility on
his shoulders to struggle alone at times. Encouraging late-
night crisis calls teaches the value of crises. (They get
results.) Giving an assignment to fulfill before the next meeting teaches responsibility and the fact that life is not a constant crisis.

You may need to discipline yourself so as not to reject or
strike back at people who display thoughtless and demanding behavior. Some people will be very good at "setting you
up" to be their "savior" by expressing a great deal of appreciation for you, by complimenting you on your decisions and
advice, and by suggesting that *no one* understands them like
you do! Nevertheless, be tolerant of such behavior; the person is usually not aware that he is fostering dependence on
you.

Even though you should be sensitive about how you introduce the idea, those you counsel should try to begin serving others. They need to move beyond their own self-pity and
pain. Losing oneself in serving others brings more solace
than anything else. It is difficult to become bogged down in
depression and self-pity while lightening the burden of
someone else.

You can do much to help those suffering from loss. Remember that they normally function well but that they are
temporarily uncertain and overwhelmed. Help the sufferer
by trying to understand his feelings and behavior without
being shocked or dismayed. Be yourself. You are the most
powerful help you have to offer.

PROBLEM-SOLVING WORKSHEET

1. Brief statement of problem:

2. Strategies (ways to solve the problem):

a.	g.	m.
b.	h.	n.
c.	i.	o.
d.	j.	p.
e.	k.	q.
f.	l.	r.

3. Decision for resolving problem:

4. Implementation:

   a. Who:

   b. When:

   c. Where:

   d. How:

5. Evaluation:

   a. Did you implement your decision? Yes _____ No _____

   b. Did the anticipated results occur: Yes _____ No _____

NOTES

1. Elisabeth Kübler-Ross, *Death—the Final Stage of Growth* (New Jersey: Prentice-Hall, 1975), p. 10.

2. M. Scott Peck, *The Road Less Traveled* (New York: Touchstone Books, 1978), p. 15.

SUGGESTED READINGS

Samuel L. Dixon, *Working With People in Crisis* (St. Louis: C.V. Mosby Co., 1979).

Viktor E. Frankl, *Man's Search for Meaning* (New York: Pocket Books, 1963).

Naomi Golan, *Treatment in Crisis Situations* (New York: The Free Press, 1978).

M. Scott Peck, *The Road Less Traveled* (New York: Touchstone Books, 1978).

ABOUT THE AUTHOR

Dr. W. Eugene Gibbons, chairman of the Social Work Department at Brigham Young University, received his bachelor's, master's, and doctor of social work degrees from the University of Utah. Dr. Gibbons has worked as a psychiatric social worker at Utah State Hospital and as director of outpatient and social services for Timpanogos Community Mental Health Center in Provo, Utah. He is presently chairman of the Utah State Board of Mental Health. He has authored several professional articles and is a member of a number of professional and honorary societies.

In the Church, Dr. Gibbons has served in a variety of callings, including bishop, stake executive secretary, YMMIA president, elders quorum president, and first counselor in a stake presidency.

He and his wife, Evelyn, are the parents of six children.

8

Self-Esteem

Terrance D. Olson and R. Lanier Britsch

Think for a moment of someone you consider confident. How would you describe him? Two qualities of confident people—noted frequently by observers—are their concern for others and their unconcern for self. In a culture where there is great concern for self-fulfillment, self-gratification, self-assertiveness, self-expression, and self-worth, it is no wonder that there is a great concern for self-esteem. However, the concept may be valuable only when making observations about *others*. If a person talks about his own self-esteem being high, listeners may see the remark as a sign of conceit.

Self-esteem is the value a person places on himself. We see only one possible value that can be an honest assessment: "And let every man esteem his brother as himself, and practise virtue and holiness before me." (D&C 38:24.)

In other words, my worth and your worth is indistinguishable. It is unnecessary to measure it, for it is infinite.

Four issues need to be considered in helping people to esteem themselves and others. First, what is our true identity? Second, what is the role of virtue and holiness—obedience—in maintaining self-esteem? Third, what do our efforts to give our best, to progress, to develop our talents and abilities, have to do with personal worth? Finally, what is the meaning of self-forgetfulness, sacrifice, and service as related to self-esteem?

Our True Identity

A person who suffers from low self-esteem often disregards his origins as a child of Heavenly Father. All of us need to know that we are unconditionally loved by God the Father and Jesus Christ. This love is not given because we are good, but because God is good. He loves all mankind, even with their faults. Latter-day Saints recognize that Christ's suffering in Gethsemane and death on Calvary were the ultimate acts of love for all people at all times.

This knowledge of our divine identity and of God's love for us is born of faith. In a sense, when accountable people discount their own infinite value, they are being unfaithful. Knowledge of truth is not sufficient for personal happiness. Acting on truth, living by it, is essential. Nevertheless, for those who see themselves as less than others, what is life like? How could their experience be described?

When people see themselves as inferior, they behave in ways that support their thinking. They are ineffective in achieving their goals. They are usually unhappy, perhaps even depressed. Mental comparisons with others give them evidence of their inadequacies. This "proof" of their shortcomings is often used as ammunition against those who would encourage them.

They may also be hesitant, shy, or hostile. Often a person with low self-esteem experiences a perverse joy at the misfortunes of those they see as superior. The overriding feeling of such people is hopelessness.

Fortunately, the gospel offers hope, but self-esteem extends beyond God's fatherhood of our spirits and his unconditional love for us. Self-esteem depends to a considerable degree on a person's ability to see himself as a productive, contributing, effective part of society. It also depends on his ability to believe that the Atonement of Christ is really valid in his behalf. This leads to the necessity of his keeping God's laws.

Obedience

Once we understand our identity, the key issue in how we

see ourselves is honesty—our obedience to what we understand. When we accept ourselves as God does, we can see our
opportunities and challenges clearly. We can meet them
with the best that is in us. We also see others honestly, and
our esteem for them matches our esteem for ourselves. The
reason this is so is that when we see ourselves honestly, we
become more godlike in our attitude toward others. Just as
God is no respecter of persons, we too become accepting
rather than unrighteously judgmental. A comparison of
people's worth is seen for what it is—a worthless activity.
The source of this kind of vision of others is our obedience to
the gospel or to whatever light and truth we have.

When a person with low self-esteem comes to you for
help, it may seem pretty simplistic just to say to them, "You
are a child of God" and "Obey the gospel." Although these
two ideas could be sources of peace and confidence for them,
in their frame of mind these ideas are seen as unrealistic.
Nevertheless, you can relate to the people by believing these
truths yourself. By accepting them as children of God, you
offer them hope and help them dispel their feelings of inadequacy. You can challenge their false beliefs about themselves.

Giving Our Best

If man now is as God once was, then man has the opportunity to progress. We claim that the keys to this progress
are knowledge and obedience. Further, we claim that effort, sacrifice, struggle, perseverance, and commitment are
fulfilling. Consequently, a person who suffers from low self-
esteem may need more than to have his beliefs challenged.
He must be challenged to act, to do, to try. "What do you
believe is possible?" is a question that invites a person to explore his faith. "What are you willing to do?" is a question
that invites him to act.

Consider this possibility. Jane is a woman who considers
herself as plain as her name. She is hesitant in public, she is
embarrassed at the Relief Society teacher training meetings
she attends, and she is so discouraged that she does not want

to teach anymore. "After all," she says, "there are so many sisters more talented than I."

Just in this brief sketch we see clues of low self-esteem:

1. A concern about how one appears to others.
2. A comparison of self with others.
3. A feeling of inadequacy.

If you were in a position to help Jane, consider the following questions:

1. Do you see her honestly, acknowledging her as a child of God? Do you see her compassionately and esteem her as yourself?

2. How would you turn her to her beliefs? With a question? ("What do you believe the Lord would have you do, Jane?" "What promptings have come to you through prayer?" "What have you learned from this struggle?" "If you were released now, how would you grow?")

Perhaps stating your beliefs would be more helpful than asking questions. ("I'm not sure releasing you would be in your best interests." "Maybe some women do have talents you don't have, but that isn't the point." "I suppose you could be released, but we need you.")

Jane's feelings should not be ignored but should be examined in the light of faith. See what she is willing to see. Tell her what you see.

3. How would you invite her to act on her faith? ("Jane, if we ask you to teach for another eight months, what are you willing to do?" "If we release you, how will that affect others? In fact, how will it affect you?" "Jane, all you can give is your best, no matter what people think.")

Such questions are meant to help Jane take responsibility, to give whatever is her best. Of course, she can discount any of these suggestions if she is insistent enough. Your responsibility is to show that faith and works will help her meet the challenges of life. Faith includes seeing her and yourself honestly and acting on that faith. You are reminding her that the "power is in [her]." (D&C 58:28.)

The foundation of these remarks is the belief that the Holy Ghost prompts the spirit of man to good acts. The human conscience also motivates to good works. And when man chooses to do right, he follows his inborn ability to act like his Father in Heaven.

When we give our best—whatever that is—it will include faith and obedience to the gospel, and some different attitudes will be evident in our lives than when we had "low self-esteem":

1. We will be concerned about our tasks and responsibilities but not about always winning the approval of others.

2. We will be concerned with giving our best and not with comparing our worth to the worth of others.

3. We will learn from our mistakes and see where we can improve.

In short, all of us are blessed with gifts or talents. All of us who are capable of worrying about self-esteem are capable of self-improvement and spiritual growth. Such growth comes through self-forgetfulness.

Self-Forgetfulness

Perhaps there is a key to appropriate counseling in the word *self-consciousness*. When we speak of a self-conscious person, we mean one who is overly concerned about how he is perceived by others or who is almost dysfunctional because of self-doubt or fear of failure. Such persons are always looking at themselves. The philosopher said, "Know thyself," but too much looking inside can shut out many other attractive landscapes.

It is significant that Moses, reflecting upon his vision of the "world upon which he was created . . . and the ends thereof, and all the children of men which are, and which were created," marveled and wondered. (Moses 1:8.)

Moses enjoyed great power in the courts of the Pharaoh, but after his vision, he remarked, "Now . . . I know that man is nothing, which thing I never had supposed." (Moses 1:10.) Such an attitude is not low self-esteem, but is humility before the glory of God. Moses also testified that because he saw the glory of God, he could discern the darkness of Satan when he came tempting Moses to worship him. Moses also recorded God's purpose for mankind: "For behold, this is my work and my glory—to bring to pass the immortality and eternal life of man." (Moses 1:39.)

God's concern is *us*, not himself. The purpose of Moses' vision was to bless Moses. God did not show his greatness for any vain purpose.

So also, in our conduct on earth, we are most blessed when we help and enrich others. If Jane is to be blessed by her Church calling, her talents, or her weaknesses, she must give up her inordinate *concern* about them and simply serve with all her faith and ability. Humility is a blessing. Feelings of inferiority are not. In rendering honest service, she could stop worrying about herself.

Since the world emphasizes the importance of the self, in one sense self-forgetfulness is an "overcoming" or a "coming out of" the world. Service given freely is, ultimately, no sacrifice at all, but this is learned only through service freely given. Then and only then will such experience teach us and be for our good. (See D&C 122.)

When Children Feel Inadequate

Children depend on adults for help in assessing the meaning of their experiences. If children are around parents and other adults who demean and reject them or in other ways refuse to love them, the children literally suffer the sins of the parents upon their heads. They learn false ideas about what family relationships should be like.

Although children come to earth to be blessed, their mistreatment can hide their blessings from them. One reason children feel inadequate is that their adequacy has never been acknowledged by the adults in their lives. Whether you are trying to help a child who feels inadequate or an adult who was sinned against as a child, neither person need be trapped by their circumstances. They can give up their feelings of inadequacy.

Your greatest help to a child in this situation is your unbridled compassion for them. You must see that they are of worth, that they need not be miserable, that their capacities for accomplishment and peace are intact. No matter what might have been done to them, they have not lost the power to be fully human. They can be free, even of the sins of their parents against them.

You will not help children by telling them these things, however. You will help them by being an example of love and truth. Fortunately, most parents are not constantly negative with their children. Most children have been treated both properly and improperly. They have been exposed to both light and darkness. Therefore, they feel inadequate only in certain situations. Still, you can provide additional light.

Children's sense of self-worth is fostered when they:

1. are talked with, not down to.
2. are asked to help someone else.
3. are appreciated for their efforts, their willingness to try.
4. care for plants, animals, and others.
5. help look for something that is lost.
6. are taught boundaries and limits.
7. are taught with love rather than harshness.
8. have adults share their wonder, fears, sorrows.
9. learn—anything.
10. are taught how to solve a problem, accomplish a task, or see how something works.
11. are included in new experiences.
12. are treated as capable people.

Esteem and Responsibility

As children grow older, their feelings of inferiority often become ways to avoid opportunities, responsibilities, or challenges. As they become accountable, such feelings can also spring from their refusal to do what they already believe is right. One high school student, who was complaining about how unfair, boring, and difficult a certain math teacher was, kept insisting that he was "no good in math." When he was told that was not true, he began insisting that he was simply no good. But he responded responsibly when asked two questions:

1. From which student in the class could you get the most
help?

2. No matter how difficult this class is, what do you yourself believe is right for you to do about it?

Suddenly, his "feelings of inadequacy" were no longer
the issue. In behaving responsibly, he no longer used such
feelings to avoid responsibility. With older children and
adults, the general principle is not to try to move them from
low self-esteem to high self-esteem, but to move them to the
point that worry about personal esteem is seen as a vain,
foolish, and irresponsible activity. Self-forgetfulness, effort,
commitment and courage are at stake. Here are some examples of ways accountable people with inferiority feelings
might give up those feelings:

Inferiority feeling: A student is embarrassed because he is
in the ninth grade and can't read.

Responsible action: The student should learn to read. He
could do this by getting help from his parents and teachers
and by practicing reading each day.

Inferiority feeling: A businessman feels that nobody at
work appreciates him.

Responsible action: He should examine his own commitment to do his best. He should strive to be of service to those
at work.

Inferiority feeling: A woman feels inadequate as she sees
that her children do not "measure up" to her neighbor's children.

Responsible action: She should teach her children that
whatever their best is, is good enough. She should teach
them what she believes is right.

Inferiority feeling: A young mother is depressed because
she quit taking music lessons as a teenager and now aches
when she hears her old college roommates play inspiring
piano pieces.

Responsible action: She should either resume learning to play the piano or learn to rejoice in the talents of her old roommates—perhaps both, if she feels these are the right things for her to do.

Inferiority feeling: Dan is not confident around those who receive the more "prominent" Church callings, and he is unhappy in his position as cubmaster.

Responsible action: Dan should yield his heart to the boys he is serving. He should pray for knowledge of how to help them and should lose himself in their service.

Inferiority feeling: A new husband feels shut out of his father-in-law's hunting and camping activities.

Responsible action: He might talk with his father-in-law about his feelings. He might also try harder to build a close relationship with his father-in-law, not because he believes this will make his father-in-law want to include him more in his activities, but because he believes it is right to be a good son-in-law.

What Else Can We Do?

In short, those among us who suffer from a poor self-image can be helped by our love for others and for ourselves. Ultimately, there is no difference between those two loves. If we acknowledge our eternal identity, we give up vain comparisons of ourselves with others and esteem them as ourselves. If we give the best in us to do what we believe is right, and if we make service and selflessness the hallmark of our relationships with others, we will see ourselves so honestly that self-esteem will not even be a concern. We will be too busy serving, blessing, and healing others to notice that we have healed ourselves. Arthur Schlesinger has noted, "When we are really honest with ourselves, we must admit that our lives are all that really belong to us. So it is how we use our lives that determines what kind of men we are. It is my deepest belief that only by giving our lives do we find life. I am convinced that the truest act of courage, the strongest act of manliness, is to sacrifice ourselves for others in a totally nonviolent struggle for justice. To be a man is to suffer for others. God help us to be men."[1]

Finally, and most appropriately, we bless those with low self-esteem when we live by the words of King Benjamin: "And behold, I tell you these things that ye may learn wisdom; that ye may learn that when ye are in the service of your fellow beings ye are only in the service of your God." (Mosiah 2:17.)

NOTE

1. Arthur M. Schlesinger, *Robert Kennedy and His Times,* vol. 2 (Boston: Houghton Mifflin Co., 1978), p. 884.

9
Managing Conflict
James T. Duke and J. Lynn England

Conflict, frustration, affliction, and misunderstanding are normal aspects of the mortal world. Speaking through Lehi, the Lord instructed us that "it must needs be, that there is an opposition in all things." (2 Nephi 2:11.) In mortality, opposition is present and makes possible choice and the exercise of agency.

This does not mean, however, that we should encourage conflict or allow it to control our lives. God expects us to improve our lives and our social relationships as much as possible during our stay in mortality, and this includes resolving conflicts and learning to develop social relationships based on love, service, patience, and understanding. (See D&C 121:41-42; Alma 7:23.) While we can expect conflict, we should also expect to manage conflict and let peace and love abound.

It is important to recognize the difference between *patterns of conflict*, in which two people (or two groups) are regularly in conflict with each other (as in sibling rivalries), and a *situational conflict* that may occur only once (as in a difference of opinion between two people who usually agree on things).

A distinction may also be made between a conflict that is accidental or unintentional and one that is intentional. How we respond to a conflict and how we go about reducing it and repairing the resulting damage to the relationship depends largely on whether the conflict was intentional or not.

The opposite of love and friendship is often identified as conflict, but the real opposite of love is indifference, apathy, and withdrawal (or divorce). As the sociologist Georg Simmel recognized, conflict is a form of association or interaction and is an indication that people care enough about their relationship to fight. As long as conflict exists, the two parties at least have a relationship, no matter how bad it may be. This conflict may lead them to hurt or even kill each other or to forgive and forget, but the conflict shows that something about the relationship is still important to the people involved. When the people show complete indifference or apathy, the relationship is dead.

This leads us to a final distinction: conflict can have both positive and negative results. Our Heavenly Father realized that opposition was an indispensable part of mortality. Conflict or competition between two people impels both to improve, strengthens group boundaries, increases the identification of group members with their own group, and forces people to establish ties with others. As muscles are strengthened by stress, so people and groups can be strengthened by conflict and tribulations. Of course, conflict often has negative results, but it may also have beneficial effects if it can be used to strengthen personal relations, negotiate more satisfactory role relationships, resolve disagreements, and so on.

Causes of Conflict

Before we can manage conflict effectively, we need to identify and understand its causes. Only if the people involved have a clear picture of the causes of conflict can they act wisely to deal with its resolution.

Individual Differences

One of the most significant causes of conflict is individual differences. People are different in many ways, and each person has a unique combination of personality and character traits. Individual differences do not necessarily lead to conflict, but they provide the potential for conflict and increase the possibility that conflict will occur. In other words, people who are similar are less likely to have conflicts than those who are different from each other. Following are discussions of some individual differences.

Physiological differences. Some of the most serious social conflicts arise from physiological differences between people, and often we are unaware of the physiological basis of such conflicts. In addition to the obvious physiological differences between males and females and old and young are many more subtle differences that influence behavior. The level of sexual desire of two marriage partners may be quite different, leading to misunderstandings and frustrations. The intelligence, manual dexterity, and energy level of people differ dramatically, and misunderstandings frequently arise from such differences. Complicating things even further, some people tend to wake up early and have their greatest energy levels in the morning hours; these are the so-called "larks." Other people, sometimes called "owls," tend to wake up later and more slowly, and their bodies take longer to reach high levels of energy. Once going, however, these individuals tend to have much higher energy levels in the evening hours and tend to stay up longer. If a "lark" is married to an "owl," or if the parents are one type while one or more of their children are another type, conflicts may arise and adjustments may be necessary. One type of person may condemn the other for being "different." What is most important is that different types of people learn to understand and appreciate each other.

Personality differences. Some people are outgoing and confident while others are more shy and quiet. Some people are aggressive or domineering while others are more submissive or adjustive. Some like adventure and others prefer security. Some people are giving while others appear to require much support from others.

Experience and conditioning. People differ greatly in the experiences they have had in their lives as well as in the way they interpret these experiences. A person who grew up in a happy home may have a totally different outlook than another person who was abused or rejected as a child. Those who have lived through a war or depression may have a very different view of the world from those who have not experienced such things.

Our experiences influence us to place greater value on some things than others and to believe that some behaviors are more successful or rewarding than others. If we are praised or rewarded for being quiet or saying our prayers, we soon learn to be quiet or say our prayers. If we gain benefits from being aggressive, we are more likely in the future to use aggression to gain our objectives. We tend to approach problems or people in ways that are customary or typical for us personally and for the members of the social group to which we belong. Thus, every person's life is a treasure trove of past experience and conditioning—a gold mine too vast to be explored or understood adequately by another person, but one we constantly return to for the resources to face our daily tasks and relationships.

Talents and interests. People differ greatly in their talents, skills, and interests. Some people appear to possess great musical ability, while others have abilities in mathematics, mechanics, or language. Some people like the opera; others like football games or boxing matches. Of course, everyone has talents and skills, but some may have a greater variety than others. Many conflicts arise from these differences. An example would be a husband who likes to attend sporting events who has a wife who would rather go to concerts.

Emotional Closeness

Emotional closeness can be a cause of conflict, but this is not often recognized. The German sociologist Georg Simmel noted that in any close relationship, it is likely that strong feelings will develop that are both positive and negative. Family members, roommates, club members, soldiers in the same outfit, and others who interact frequently are likely to develop strong feelings toward each other. Usually these are feelings of affection and friendship that contribute to the well-being of the group and the happiness of its members. However, such emotional closeness can lead also to misunderstanding, frustration, competition, and anger. Frequently, close relationships involve a mixture of positive *and* negative feelings. Spouses are likely to feel both love and frustration more strongly with each other than with a casual acquaintance. After all, they interact more frequently, and their relationship touches every facet of their lives.

Several years ago the sleeping arrangements in one family placed a thirteen-year-old boy in the same bedroom with his three-year-old brother. The parents noted that these two brothers of different ages developed a strong affection for each other and that the elder brother cared for and helped his younger brother. In turn, the younger boy sought out the elder brother when he needed help. However, these two boys were also more likely than other children in the family to quarrel and to feel frustrated with each other about such things as cleaning up their room.

Police have long been aware that family squabbles tend to escalate into violence more frequently than other types of misunderstandings. And social occasions, especially in the local tavern, are more likely to produce both friendship and violent confrontations. Many parents have noted that when the emotional level in the home gets high and people are laughing, teasing, and getting excited, misunderstandings and squabbles may also occur. They therefore try to keep the emotional level on a more even keel to help control conflict.

Expectations and Norms

Every person has a great diversity of expectations about how various people will behave. From experience I have come to expect my seventeen-year-old son to show joy when a bowl of ice cream is placed before him and to reject a bowl of peas.

Such expectations tend to be communicated from person to person and to become standardized within a social group—both my wife and I share the same expectations about the reactions of our son to certain foods. When such expectations are widely shared within a social group, they become a social norm, a group-held expectation of behavior. Such norms serve as standards of behavior and tend to be infused with a moral character, so that people expect others to act in a certain way and believe that they *should* act that way. Sometimes these norms are enacted into law, but more frequently they are simply communicated from person to person and sanctioned informally. Many norms apply only to a specific type of person, for example, to a young man, a wife, or a doctor. As people grow up, they learn the norms of their social group and society and "internalize" or accept as their own these norms. People carry these norms in their minds and apply them to themselves and others constantly. For example, college professors are expected to stand up while they lecture; college students are expected to sit down and take notes. Mothers "should" do the dishes; fathers "should" mow the lawn. Children "should" obey their parents. People "should" go to church on Sunday.

Conformity to the expectations of others is much more extensive than nonconformity. We eat the food typical of our group (whether pasta or potatoes), sleep early or late as is the custom, wear clothing dictated by social custom, and follow the latest fads in diets or exercise or recreation. We stand in line without crowding in, speak when we are spoken to, cut our meat with a knife, and don't eat with our fingers. The expectations of others, especially those who are close to us, have a powerful impact on our lives.

Some norms carry a stronger moral tone than others, and some norms (like those regarding sex roles) may not be agreed upon by everyone. And the strength of norms tends to decline as people choose not to conform to the norm and act contrary to the expectations of others.

One of the greatest sources of conflict in social relationships is disagreement about norms or nonconformity to group-held expectations. If a young man grows up in a group that teaches the norm of male aggressiveness and independence and then marries a young woman who learned a different expectation of male responsibility and quiet leadership, both the man and the woman may feel that the other person is not living up to his or her expectations.

In my family as I was growing up, my mother always took out the garbage after a meal and put it in a garbage can in our garage. In my wife's family, her father always carried the garbage out of the house. When we were married, we both expected the other to carry out the garbage. What is most significant about this example, however, is that we did not communicate our expectations to each other. We simply had come to assume that certain things would happen, and we were both uncomfortable that the other was not living up to our expectations. Since we loved each other, we didn't want to criticize each other, so without speaking about the garbage we both waited for the other to take it out, and eventually one or the other of us would, all the while muttering under his breath. Only when the conflict became more marked did one of us mention it to the other; then we were able to discuss our expectations openly. Eventually, buying a garbage disposal solved much of the problem, and now we both take an equal responsibility to put the garbage down the disposal.

Only by bringing their expectations to the surface and discussing them openly can people deal with them. But we should realize that norms may have been long internalized and that it is not easy to change one's norms once they are well established.

Sin

Breaking God's commandments—that is, sinning—lies at the root of much of the world's conflict and unhappiness. Alma told his wayward son, Corianton, "Wickedness never was happiness." (Alma 41:10.) Mormon identified Satan as the "author of all sin" (Helaman 6:30), and in his great sermon to his son Jacob, Lehi said that because Satan "had fallen from heaven, and had become miserable forever, he sought also the misery of all mankind" (2 Nephi 2:18). The Savior taught that "the spirit of contention . . . is of the devil." (3 Nephi 11:29.)

It follows that one of the best ways to avoid conflict is to be righteous and obedient and to practice the law of love in our relationships with others. People who are guided by the

Spirit, who are "full of charity towards all men," and who "let virtue garnish [their] thoughts unceasingly" (D&C 121:45) do not enter into conflict with others. Of course, they may sometimes "[reprove] . . . with sharpness," which may set the person in conflict with the person he has reproved, but the relationship is strengthened because the person "show[s] forth afterwards an increase of love toward him whom [he has] reproved." (D&C 121:43.)

Sin may be a source of conflict when people do not agree on what is sinful. At a restaurant a woman orders a cola drink. Her husband sees this as breaking the Word of Wisdom, and conflict ensues. On Sunday a boy plays a sandlot baseball game with members of his deacons quorum, and his mother accuses him of breaking the Sabbath.

Resolving Conflicts

Resolving conflicts usually involves at least four things: changing how we think, changing how we feel, changing our behavior, and changing our relationships. Social scientists often speak of the ABCs of social life: (a) affect (emotion), (b) behavior, and (c) cognition (thinking). To these three might be added a fourth: relationships. These elements are central to understanding human behavior and how conflicts may be resolved. A change in any one of these elements will bring changes in the others because of their close interconnection. Changing our way of thinking will bring about a change in our emotions, our behavior, and our relationships. Likewise, changing behavior will bring about a change in feeling and thinking. Consequently, conflict can often be resolved through changes in feelings, behavior, thinking, or relationships.

Once the cause of a conflict has been identified, it is much easier to decide how to resolve the conflict. Following are discussions of various techniques to help resolve conflicts.

Toleration: A Change in Thinking and Feeling

One of the best ways to deal with conflict is to tolerate it and the differences that underlie it. Rather than being upset that his wife thinks differently than he does, a husband might accept the difference and come to appreciate the variety and interest it creates in his life. Differences can be a source of strength in a relationship. If one spouse is a "lark" and the other is an "owl," for example, each spouse will have some time alone to read, think, or write.

Repentance: A Change in Behavior

Some conflicts can be resolved through repentance. Sometimes only one person in a relationship has sinned and needs repentance. But more frequently, both need to repent. A truly repentant attitude can resolve the pain of the person who has sinned and, provided the other person is forgiving, bring their relationship back to one of peace and harmony.

Forgiveness

Our Heavenly Father expects us to forgive those who have sinned against us. (See D&C 64:10.) Much conflict arises or is prolonged because we fail to heed this counsel. When we carry bad feelings in our hearts, when we condemn others and refuse to forgive them, we unnecessarily add fuel to a conflict and keep it going long after it should have been resolved.

It usually takes two people to fight. In our family we have learned that when a person refuses to be offended, or when a person forgives quickly, the conflict is soon resolved and peace is restored. It is possible for one person to keep a conflict going if he persists in offending or hurting another, but most people will turn from their sins if the other person forgives and refuses to join the conflict. When we truly forgive, we remember the sin no more and treat the person who has sinned against us as if nothing had happened.

My three-year-old daughter taught me such forgiveness. I had been impatient and unloving with her on a Saturday night and had sent her to bed with some harsh words. The next morning I left for Church meetings that lasted most of the morning. During this time I felt sorry for my actions of the previous night and planned to ask my daughter's forgiveness. I finally arrived at our ward near the close of our sacrament meeting. Upon entering the building, I found my daughter sitting in the foyer on her elder sister's lap. I sat down beside them, and as I did so, my younger daughter slid onto my lap and settled in comfortably. She didn't say a word, but she gave me no sign that she remembered my harshness. I held her in my arms, I felt forgiven and healed of my sin, and our relationship was restored.

Negotiation and Compromise

Most people resolve their conflicts through negotiation, but they do not usually realize that they are negotiating. Raising children involves a continual sequence of proposals by parent or child and counter-proposals by the other. Living together as husband and wife requires the repeated use of suggestions and counter-suggestions about individual conduct and family activities. However, most of us do not recognize that we are negotiating. Rarely do we plan our negotiating strategy and devote as much time to negotiating with our spouses and children as we do to negotiating with a car salesman or real estate broker. Yet, the consequences of negotiations within the family last longer and affect our lives more than any purchase or passing relationship.

When family members begin to search for ways to improve their abilities as negotiators, they need to understand the nature of family relationships. First, negotiations to solve any single conflict take place as part of relationships that have usually had a long history of negotiations and face an equally long future. They are not like negotiations with a salesman we have never met before and will probably never see again. Hence, as we negotiate, that history and future need to be taken into account. Second, the family relationship is one that involves virtually every aspect of our lives. We know many things about each other that are irrelevant to the current conflict. We know personal items that can hurt the person with whom we are negotiating. There may be several other areas of conflict that have not yet been resolved.

Consequently, as we negotiate with family members it is tempting to bring up other problems to hurt the other person. Third, as we seek models of good negotiators and effective strategies for negotiations, it is important to remember that the other party is not a hated enemy, does not have goals that are very different from our own, and is not going to be able to go home after negotiations are over.

These characteristics of family relationships lead us to emphasize three aspects of negotiations. First, negotiation is a way to solve conflicts to ensure that all who are involved benefit in some way. The basic idea behind negotiations is that a careful consideration of all alternatives should lead to a settlement that is an improvement for everyone over the existing situation. The problem is not who will give in, but how much each person must compromise to promote mutual benefit.

The second aspect of family negotiation is that negotiations must be focused on a specific issue and the strategies used must be restricted to protect the relationship. When a husband and wife are negotiating over the frequency of visits to in-laws, it does not ordinarily help to bring up other unresolved issues such as appropriate Sunday activities while on vacation, techniques for disciplining a teenage daughter, or the current method of meeting family financial obligations. Typically, this only adds one more unresolved issue to the list. In addition, it is often tempting to use knowledge about the other person's weaknesses and emotions to obtain a favorable solution or to coerce him into a concession. For example, if a husband wants to visit his parents more frequently, and his wife knows he feels guilty about his inability to stand up to his parents' excessive demands, the wife may be tempted to keep the number of visits as they are simply by attacking his masculinity and pointing out the childish nature of his desires. His guilt may need to be worked out at some point, but it is destructive to use it on him in this way.

The final aspect of negotiations in families is that they need to be based on mutual trust. A friend once described a disagreement with her husband in which he agreed to give up a football game to attend the wedding of a member of her family. She said, "He gave in so easily that I knew he was up to something. I am scared to death that he plans to use this on me to get me to do something I really don't like." Negotiations between persons who don't trust each other are greatly complicated by the guessing involved in trying to determine what the other person is really planning or meaning. A Jewish anecdote describes this problem: "Telling me you are going to Minsk so that I will think you are going to Pinsk helps me to know that you will go to Minsk." People who are starting to resolve conflict by improving their negotiating skills must examine the trust in their relationship. If trust is low, the first order of business should be increasing trust.

It is helpful to think of negotiation as a three-stage process: (1) information gathering and issue formation, (2) bargaining, (3) agreement.

Most effective negotiators start out by seeking information and trying to clarify the issue. During this phase of the negotiations, it is important to avoid taking firm positions or forcing the other parties to take firm positions. Background information about the feelings of all the parties, their thoughts, and their actions are crucial. Find out where you are and where the others are. This will be extremely helpful in conducting the other phases of the negotiations. If I know that my daughter is feeling socially insecure and is afraid of being left out of social events, I will be much more skillful and considerate as we negotiate whether she will baby-sit or attend a school dance.

Similarly, background concerning the state of the relationship is extremely important. When a wife and her husband resolve a conflict over the frequency of visits to in-laws, the alternatives considered, offers made, and reactions to suggestions may depend on the kind of relationship between them. What are the communication patterns (open, closed, or restricted)? Is the relationship healthy or in trouble?

Finally, a negotiator should clarify the issues to be negotiated. Each person should state as clearly as possible the issues that raise the current problem. This is important because it focuses the discussion on specifics instead of allowing matters to remain general and vague. It also helps the people to know each other's concerns. Too often negotiations fail because, unknowingly, the parties are responding to different issues.

The second stage involves the actual exchange of offers or suggestions. The various alternatives are presented and responded to. Some alternatives are eliminated because they are mutually unacceptable or totally undesirable for one of the parties. Other alternatives are retained for further consideration. The basic question when an alternative is presented is whether the listening party should make a concession and modify some aspect of his position by moving closer to agreement with the other. People often fear making concessions because they are afraid of looking weak. However, concessions are extremely important in convincing the other person to compromise as well. Some modest concessions should be made early, but they should be accompanied by an explanation of the expectations of concessions from the others involved. A father might suggest to his daughter, "I am willing to have you go to your school party this Saturday instead of tending the younger children if you will tend them next Friday night."

In addition to presenting alternatives, each person should respond to each suggestion to formulate new alternatives. The final solution to a conflict is often created during the negotiations. Some refer to this as seeking the formula to solve the problem. As my daughter and I negotiate over her activities on weekends, the ultimate solution may be a new suggestion arising from our reactions to earlier alternatives.

The exchanges of alternatives and attempts to create new alternatives usually lead to an agreement. As the agreement is reached, it should be implemented with care, for two reasons. First, everyone needs to feel that he gained from the process. Second, the agreement reached on a specific issue lays the foundations for the subsequent negotiations. It is important to make certain that the trust and quality of the relationship have held constant or have improved. When agreements are implemented with care, the true strengths of negotiation emerge: the conflict is resolved, the parties are better off, and the relationship is improved.

Mediation

At times none of the tactics described above resolve a conflict. If the issue is not serious, we usually learn to live with the lack of agreement. However, at other times the issue is serious or it introduces other conflicts that are not solved either. The failure may arise due to a lack of trust, intolerance, failure to repent, failure to forgive, or other problems. In any case, the people involved need to look outside themselves for a solution. In formal conflict resolution, a mediator is often brought in as a disinterested third party. In families, this strategy is often useful. A mediator can be brought in to help the family explore their feelings, thinking, and actions to try to find opportunities for change. The relationship may be examined for ways to improve it. A mediator is often most helpful simply as a source of new alternatives. The couple trying to solve the issue of in-law visits may never have explored inviting in-laws to their home, changing the format of the visits, or using the telephone. A mediator may simply provide such fresh ideas.

The choice of a mediator is crucial. It must be someone who is not more closely allied to one of the parties than the other. A husband's tennis companion is probably not a good choice because he will be seen by the wife simply as an ally of her husband. The person may also be someone who is personally interested in both parties and who can be talked to openly by them. Sometimes bishops, Relief Society presidents, teachers, or friends ably perform the role.

Conclusion

Conflict is a normal part of living. However, an understanding of the nature of a conflict, an appreciation for its underlying causes, and using techniques to manage it can make our lives more pleasant and less stressful.

ABOUT THE AUTHORS

Dr. James T. Duke, professor of sociology at Brigham Young University, received his bachelor's and master's degrees from the University of Utah and his Ph.D. from the University of California at Los Angeles. He has taught at UCLA, the University of Utah, and the University of Texas at El Paso. In 1971, Dr. Duke received the Professor of the Year Award for distinguished teaching at BYU.

Dr. Duke presently serves as a high councilor in the Orem, Utah, Sharon Stake. He has previously served as a branch president at BYU, as stake and ward YMMIA president, as stake and ward Sunday School president, and as elders quorum instructor. He has done research on conversion for the Correlation Evaluation Department of the Church.

He and his wife, Ruth, are the parents of nine children.

Dr. J. Lynn England, professor of sociology at Brigham Young University, received his bachelor's and master's degrees in philosophy from the University of Utah and his Ph.D. in sociology from the University of Pittsburgh. He has taught at BYU since 1970. His special interests are the sociology of knowledge and mediation and negotiation. He has published widely and is a member of several honorary and professional associations.

Dr. England has served as a teacher in various organizations of the Church, as a member of a stake Sunday School presidency, and as first counselor in the bishopric of his Orem ward.

He and his wife, Anna, are the parents of five children.

10

Counseling Couples
Terrance D. Olson

Fundamental to successful marriage counseling is the belief that progress is possible with any couple. When you don't believe change is possible, it is time to do something other than counsel the couple. You could refer them to professional help, of course, or you could simply acknowledge that you believe you have nothing to offer.

Fortunately, many options are available to pursue before your personal and spiritual resources are exhausted. There are numerous steps, conditions, and strategies to consider *before* you get to the end of your rope.

In counseling a couple, you must have faith that change *can* occur. You need not be professionally trained to exercise faith. Nor must you be licensed to hold before a couple, however dark their despair, the *hope* that they can overcome their problems.

Who Should Be Present in Counseling?
Typically, you can help even when one member of the couple refuses to visit you. When this is true, however, or when one partner wants the meetings to be kept secret from the other, success is unlikely. Such restrictions suggest that one or both partners do not feel "at one" with the other. But if you listen to one partner's story, you have a one-eyed view of the marriage. You may begin to make the same judgments against the missing member of the marriage that the person telling you about the marriage is making. You then become

an ally of the person you are counseling, not a counselor who is going to foster change or strengthen a marriage.

The solution to this problem is rarely to see one partner and then the other. It may look as if you could be more "fair" if you "heard both sides," but you will only have heard two jaundiced views of the relationship instead of one. You then place yourself (with the couple's assistance) in the position of judging the credibility of each partner in the marriage instead of helping them.

In most cases where the marriage *relationship* seems to be the problem, you cannot even begin to suggest solutions until the couple attend the counseling sessions together. This does not mean that one person cannot be taught, but it does mean if one partner in a marriage is deeply troubled about the relationship, involving the other partner is fundamental to solving their relationship problems.

Seeing the Couple

Although the couple appears for help together, one or both partners may be reluctant to take responsibility or to address issues directly. It is helpful to ask each partner why they have come and what they hope to accomplish. In this way you focus on a goal, a possibility, a direction.

Here's an example:

Counselor:	What do you hope our time together will accomplish?
Husband:	I don't know. She's the one who is upset and drag—uh—wanted us to come.
Wife (looking at husband):	Maybe you had better tell him why I get upset.
Husband:	You're a big girl, you tell him.
Wife:	Oh, you never want to help with *anything*, do you?
Husband:	(Exhales slowly.)
Wife:	We just don't seem to get along, we—
Husband:	She just doesn't like the fact that I'd rather be in the bowling league once a month than stay home with her every night.
Wife:	Is *that* what you think? Well, you can go bowling every night if you want. Don't let me keep you around your own house and your own kids.

Counselor:	I'm willing to have either one of you tell me, before we go any further, what you would like the future to be like. I'd rather have you look ahead to some goal or dream.
Wife:	I don't know if I have any dreams anymore. (Glances at husband.)
Husband:	(Exhales slowly.)

Negativism, veiled put-downs, reined resentment, accusations, martyr-like complaints, and superiority through silence are reasonable descriptions of the "mood" of this couple. Notice that this couple has used the lay counselor's two invitations to identify a hope or goal to "get at" each other. It is usually safe to assume that even in this brief conversation, the couple has revealed a pattern and theme of their interaction at home.

So what do you do? There are two things you ought *not* to do: (1) Do not listen to rehearsals of the two sides of their story; and (2) do not sketch for this couple reminders of what it means to be one in marriage or note what they ought to be like. Most couples who are this accusatory have magnified their problems to the point that it affects almost every aspect of their lives. Moreover, each partner is usually blind to his role in fueling the fires of hostility and destructiveness. Consequently, if you intervene and ask them to "tell their story" in an orderly way (by taking turns for example), you may formalize and legitimize the hostile and destructive interactions you have already witnessed.

Likewise, when people are having marital difficulties, the experience of being "one" in marriage is foreign to them. Even though they are seeking help, they do not correctly imagine how they would feel or what their life would be like if they were free of their problems. Therefore, your suggestions may be seen by the people in distress as unrealistic fantasies.

Whose Responsibility Is the Problem?

This couple have avoided taking responsibility for a solution to their problem. They may not know what their problem is or what the possible solutions are, but that does not make it impossible for them to ponder both causes and consequences of their behavior. The counselor's goal is to place responsibility for the healing of their marriage on their shoulders. This will help bring the oneness in their relationship that now seems an unlikely option.

How do you place responsibility? Here are some suggestions:

1. *Give direct instruction.* Explain that whatever new behaviors or changes the couple wants, both the responsibility for and the power to achieve them are in their hands.

> *Counselor:* I've asked you a couple of times to share with me a goal or direction you wish to pursue, but you have done something else. What is it you wish me to understand about your coming here? (This is another invitation to focus on the issues.)
>
> *or*
>
> I believe you have the ability to work this out, but right now you seem to be using your ability to hurt rather than help each other. (Explain your belief in their capacity to improve.)
>
> *or*
>
> If I listen to the complaints each of you has right now, what am I supposed to do, choose sides? It almost looks as if you want me to be a referee instead of a counselor. (This is a description of what might be the outcome of listening to complaints. Making a statement like this followed by silence leaves the ball in their court. It is now their responsibility to initiate something.)

2. *Teach principles of righteous living.* Sometimes people understand their responsibility if they are reminded of some truth they claim to believe in.

> *Counselor:* Do you believe in agency—the power in you to meet challenges that come your way?
> *Couple:* Yes.
> *Counselor:* Are there also some moral truths you believe in?
> *Couple:* I guess so.
> *Counselor:* Then could we proceed in this way? If each of you were to accept the idea that you could do some things

differently to help improve your relationship, then we could tackle first things first. Each of you, no matter what the wrongs of the other against you might be, could focus on what *you* could do, rather than on what the other has done.

Couple: But what if I change and my partner doesn't?

Counselor: What if each of you demands that the other change before you do? What then? (There will be no change.)

By the way, the only kind of change I'm talking about right now is that you exercise your agency to live by things you believe in.

Let's consider what might have happened if the answer to the first question—"Do you believe in agency?"—had been negative.

Couple: Yes, I believe in agency, but a person can take only so much.

Counselor: In other words, your partner's insensitivities or sins have made it impossible for you to meet life, to change, or to be happy?

Couple: Well . . .

Counselor: If you really are trapped by each other, what hope is there for either of you? Wasn't seeking help or coming here something you did on your own?

Husband: Well, yes, but she put a lot of pressure on me.

Counselor: What I am getting at is this: I believe you have the power to have your marriage be different. If *you* don't believe that, coming here is futile, because I can only invite you to examine your hearts. If you are not willing to look, what will we accomplish?

Teaching principles (like personal responsibility) is important because it is your way of bringing a couple face to face with possibilities. It also often reveals inconsistencies or flaws in the way they see their current situation.

3. *Invite obedience to what they believe.* There is a difference between what people believe in and what they insist on when they are taking offense from their partner. In the initial dialogue, it was shown that the couple was more interested in baiting each other than in addressing the issue they supposedly came to resolve.

In placing responsibility, you are sowing seeds of change

in the proper field. In teaching principles, you are establishing a foundation for mutual action. In inviting obedience, you are asking the couple to focus on their own responsibilities, sometimes even in spite of what each person is doing. You need not hide what you are doing from the couple, and you could share with them any ground rules you wish to abide by. For example:

> *Counselor:*   This may not be what you expected, but I would like
> to institute the Golden Rule here in our discussions.
> That is, I would like all of us to treat each other as we
> would like to be treated.

When you as a counselor move along these lines, you set the stage for success. All three of these recommendations (place responsibility, teach principles, and invite obedience) strike at the heart of any matter. In addition, you establish a mood and atmosphere in which the counseling can proceed, which is itself a model of the kind of atmosphere necessary for this couple to resolve difficulties on their own. An hour discussing disagreements, misunderstandings—even past hostilities—in a spirit guided by the Golden Rule may not be an overnight cure, but it is a powerful live demonstration of another way to live.

When People Refuse to Be Responsible

Professional counselors are often amazed at the intensity of the blaming, argumentative attitudes of the people who come seeking help. The sheer energy required to maintain such a high level of hate, moment after moment, is great. People in such conditions seem, because of their perspective and their emotions, to be incapable of changing. Most of the time, however, such perspectives and emotions are not the cause of the problem, they *are* the problem. Many times the resentments, hostilities, and depressions of the help-seekers, though really felt by them, have a different origin than they suppose.

Usually they think that the insensitivity of their partner, or the financial pressures of a large family, or their own low self-esteem is the source of their "uncontrollable" feelings, but it may be that these very feelings are the evidence a troubled person clings to as "proof" of how they are wronged, mistreated, or incompetent. Even if this view is logical to you, it is unlikely that "diagnosing" the people who come to you would be well received.

That is why I have suggested that in a context of love and faith you establish general boundaries for the counseling. These boundaries are actually a way of establishing a starting point for change. The couples you help must have a willingness to ponder, to take personal responsibility, and to have a forgiving heart, a repentant spirit, a confessing soul. Sometimes establishing this beginning can take weeks. But persist! Until the couple gives up their destructive attitudes, you can do little to help them. To give up such destructive feelings does not mean to express, vent, control, or stifle them. It means to give them up. When people think that such feelings cannot be given up, they are limiting the success of the counseling sessions.

Negative, nonproductive, hateful feelings can be given up, even though the person feeling them might laugh at such an idea. Only after the feelings have been given up is it completely evident that they can be. Ruptures in marriages can be healed, but healing them starts with compassionately confronting the attitudes by which couples make enemies of one another.

What Is Your Responsibility as a Counselor?

Your responsibility is to show the couple that they have the capacity to change. If you see the possibility of their change, if you care about the people who come to you, then you have found a starting point to help them. That starting point is not something reserved for those who are trained as marriage and family counselors. It is grounded in who you are as a person. Your success as a counselor depends more on what kind of man or woman you are than on what formal knowledge you have. The compassionate, firm, truth-telling friend can be more powerful than any professional who is devoid of these qualities.

Avoiding "Diagnosis"

Sometimes counselors and couples get caught up in the complexity of "diagnosis," of exploring extensive whys and wherefores of attitudes, predicaments, or behavior patterns. Guessing the reasons for behavior may be a part of the approach a counselor takes. However, it may be counter-productive to give a couple an analysis of their behavior.

Teaching people to analyze each other does not free them of their miseries; it simply allows them to continue their ac-cusatory feelings toward each other on a more sophisticated, analytical level. There is an old story about a man who had sought counseling as a remedy for his emotional misery. After months of counseling sessions, the man seemed to his friends to be as miserable as before. When asked how things were progressing, he responded, "Well, I feel much better." When told that he seemed just as unhappy as before, he re-plied, "Oh, I am still as miserable as I ever was, but now I know why." As a helper of couples you should not become a party to that kind of solution.

Here's an example. Let's suppose that the "reason" Julie is hesitant to give compliments to her husband is "because" her own father mistreated her, or "because" her husband does not appreciate her. If this analysis is correct, then Julie is seen as a victim, either of her father's treatment of her or of her husband's current attitude. Since her father is present only in her past, we turn to her husband with the idea of teaching him to be more appreciative of her. We explain her "need" for his approval. He complains that he could be more appreciative of her if only she would quit being so impatient and negative with the children. He agrees to "try" to praise her, but confides that this is going to require some energy and searching of her behavior to find something praise-worthy. He also explains how afraid he always was of his mother, who spoke to her children harshly.

In other words, we have a husband and wife who see their behavior as the result of what is being "done unto them" by the other. "If only he were more appreciative, I could then relate to him," thinks Julie. "If only she weren't so negative, I would, of course, be able to reward her," thinks Phil. Each believes himself to be a victim of the other. Each is trapped. Each thinks he or she is forced, *by the other's behavior,* to feel and do what he or she is doing and feeling.

What do we accomplish with such a couple if we explain their behavior to them by using their own perspective? We justify their actions and agree to their helplessness. Especially if we promote the notion that they are victims of their *parents'* behavior do we then become part of the problem. Then we see them as victims of their past, rather than as agents who could be free of whatever negative experiences might have been theirs.

There is a second reason not to spend time on extensive analyses or explanations. By teaching a couple to be analytical about each other, we may be inviting them to see each other as objects, to look for hidden motives, to second-guess the "meaning" behind their mate's behavior in ways that encourage them to stay apart.

Seeking Honesty

The better way would be for each partner to examine his or her willingness to "yield his heart" to the other. This would include a discussion of what each believes is *right* to do, whether or not the partner is also doing right. Each should ponder what kind of person he can and ought to be. This will help them focus on their own attitudes, thus striking at the root of what keeps them distant from each other.

As the impatient woman examines her own behavior, she considers what her relationship with her children (and her husband) would be like if she were less tense or ruffled. After all, though her impatience is a "bone of contention," she is not that way all the time. By imagining the times when she is giving and calm, she reminds herself that she does experience something other than constant tension.

Similarly, however unappreciative this husband might be, he can remember his times of freely giving and caring. By considering the difference in his relationship with his wife when he *is* appreciative, he can imagine the world of experience he would like to live in with her.

Sometimes marriage partners examine their own attitudes as a way of showing that their attitudes are not their fault. They insist that they are trapped by what their partner is like. Again, if they are right, if they really are trapped, what hope is there for change?

We cannot decide what others are going to do, but we can decide what we are going to do. If a feuding couple will not accept this idea, *they will persist in using their agency to insist that they have none.*

This stalemate means there will be no progress toward a solution of the couple's problems. For the couple who have been taught to find explanations or "reasons" for their feelings, it means a justification of their problem, not an escape from it.

The wife in our example may begin thinking about her husband in this way: "He just can't relate to women, given what his mother was like. I don't know what I'm going to do. If that's who he is, that's who he is."

The husband, of course, may be thinking, "She just doesn't have the constitution to handle children. Boy, it's going to be a tense fifteen more years."

Contrast these attitudes with these alternatives:

Wife:	I will be my best. If I stumble, I stumble, but I can always keep trying. Besides, I know I don't have to take offense at what he does.
Husband:	I guess sometimes things don't go well with her. I wonder if there is anything I could do to help when I come home?

The truth is, *we cannot make people change.* So the obvious question is, how do we move people from their nega-

tive attitudes to more caring ones? We can invite them to do
so, we can sketch the alternative way of living, but until
people acknowledge *their own role* in their difficulties, they
will remain in them.

Compassionate, understanding attitudes are what provide a foundation for solutions to the kinds of problems illustrated here, and those attitudes are the responsibility of the
people who hold them. The alternative to diagnosing a
couple, then, is to teach them general principles of relationships while placing responsibility for change on their shoulders.

Pointing Out Patterns

It is often helpful to point out to a couple the patterns of
behavior they are cooperating to produce. You are asking
them to see something outside themselves (a pattern of relating to each other), but in a way that helps them realize
that they are generating the pattern.

By observing them as they interact together, you will discover patterns of behavior. If the couple fails to respond to
your questions about why they have come to you, you can always ask them to describe some part of their relationship—
how they handle financial matters, what they believe about
child rearing, or how they plan holiday activities. Observe
carefully. Do not make too much out of little things (such as
who responds first, who defers to whom, etc.), but look for
repetitive patterns. (Does one partner frequently interrupt
the other? Does a challenge from one partner usually result
in silence from the other?)

Let's assume that the couple has been dealing with an
issue as if it were a "hot potato." That is, each makes a comment that throws responsibility on the partner to answer a
question or disclose feelings. This may occur when a couple
begins to answer one of your questions:

Husband (to
wife):   Well, why don't you go ahead?
Wife: No, that's okay—go on.
Husband: Well, I think you have stronger feelings about it.

Wife:	But you're the one who thinks I'm not doing it right.
Husband:	Yes, but he needs to have your point of view.
Wife:	Maybe, but you go first; you brought us here.

And so it goes. This is a pattern *you* could analyze if you wanted to, but a more effective way to help the couple would be to show them their pattern and let *them* tell you what it might mean. In practice, before you point out a pattern you would want the couple to show you more examples of this pattern than just this beginning dialogue.

Counselor:	I've noticed a way that you two are cooperating that you may not be aware of.
Husband:	What do you mean?
Counselor:	I notice that each of you invites the other to speak first.
Wife:	Well, maybe so, but so what?
Counselor:	I'm not sure, but I'm wondering what that means to you. For example, if you two were trying to make a decision about something and this were the pattern you were using, how would you come to a decision?
Wife:	I guess sometimes we do hesitate a long time.
Counselor:	And that may be valuable, and you can talk about that after you leave here, but there is something else about this pattern that teaches me something about you—you cooperate very well to produce such a pattern. It could not exist without both of you "working at it," so to speak. In other words, I know you have the ability to cooperate. The question to consider may be "How often do you cooperate in positive or negative ways?"
Husband:	Well, I don't see what this has to do with our problem.
Counselor:	Maybe nothing. You'll have to think it out.
Husband:	Then why are you telling us all this?
Counselor:	So I can learn from you what you understand about yourselves.
Wife:	Well, we don't know about these kinds of things.
Counselor:	But you know enough about your own family to be able to discuss this with each other.

When should you point out a pattern? Usually when you feel doing so would achieve the following purposes:

1. When the pattern you are observing is destructive to the couple's relationship.

2. When the couple's pattern is not addressing the appropriate issue (they come in to discuss finances and start moaning about the husband's unjust boss).

3. When the couple is united in blaming people or factors outside themselves for their troubles.

It is important not to assign motives to the patterns you describe. That is just analysis again. Your goal is to help the couple see their own role in their problem and that they may be maintaining the problem through the way they "cooperate."

Examining Beliefs

If the couple does not agree on what marital commitment means and what beliefs partners in a marriage should have, counseling them may accomplish little. However, these beliefs do not necessarily have to be presented in the counseling sessions. They may be, but the most important examination of beliefs would be each marriage partner's reflection on his or her own commitments, values, and standards. This could be done through private reflection, personal journal writing, pondering and prayer, or talking with the marriage partner outside the counseling session.

The purpose of examining beliefs is to clarify what the person's commitments are. For example, does Julie believe in the value of impatience as a way to deal with children, promote family unity, and so on? Does Phil really believe it right to withhold appreciation from his wife? These may seem like ridiculous questions to a couple who think their impatience or lack of appreciation is not their fault, but the issue is to acknowledge what the standard is, what the hope or dream for the future is. Sometimes, when a husband or wife is complaining about his or her mate, you can ask this, "Do you believe that what you are doing in this situation is right?" The person may not be able to give an answer, but it may only be necessary for the person to ponder the question to change his blaming or negative attitude. When people are feeling or behaving in ways they do not believe are right, little permanent change is likely until they give up what goes against what

they believe. Suppose a woman is complaining about her alcoholic husband. Her rehearsal of his wrongs may be accurate—his disappearing for a day, his late-night stumbling
through the door, his verbal abuse of the children. However,
to help this woman deal effectively with her husband's problem, you must first make sure that she is not *part* of the problem.

For example, imagine that this woman's discouragement
becomes apparent to her friends. They try to buoy her up, to
encourage her. At first she appreciates the love and concern
of her friends. But as time passes, she becomes more and
more dependent on their sympathy. This dependence, if it is
to continue, requires that her husband continue in his problem. In other words, the woman is now dependent not only
on her friends' support but on her husband's alcoholism. If
so, she must give up her attitude, which helps maintain, not
eliminate, her husband's problem. To solve the problem, she
will have to adopt a new attitude toward him—compassion
and concern (assuming this is what she believes is right). She
will have to give up being a helpless victim of his wrongdoing. This may require firm behavior from her, including
her refusal to "bail him out" of his self-produced miseries.
However, such firmness may be a powerful act of love that
invites him to become responsible. Her alternative—to sit
back as a martyr and receive a perverse comfort from
others—shows neither respect for herself nor love for her
husband. In such a condition, the marriage is not a blessing
to either partner.

Asking Questions

In a way, asking people what they believe is right is a
measure of their willingness to learn from you and a sign of
how honest they are willing to be. Asking such a question
will either be accepted or resisted, but you may not know the
outcome of asking the question until weeks have passed.
Therefore, if your question does not seem to invite an honest
reflection or personal searching, *do not* follow it up with
more pushing or challenging questions. The value of the

question consists, in part, in backing away after you have asked it. By asking the question, you have invited them to turn their attention to an issue more fundamental than their complaints. You have also placed the responsibility on their shoulders to examine other possible ways of seeing the situation.

The question of what a couple believes is right is not the only question that could be asked. Here are some others:

1. "If your current problems were solved, what would your marriage be like for you?" This question invites the couple to imagine a future different from the present. Their answer may reveal important hopes or goals, but the most important clues for you are emotional ones. As they answer this question, do they have an attitude of hope? Do they agree at all regarding what their marriage would be like if it were in good condition? Are they somewhat determined to bring their expectations to pass?

2. "What strengths do you have as a couple that could be used to help you solve this problem?" Often, couples in conflict are so busy insisting how bad things are that they deny that their abilities could alter the situation. By shifting their concern from their problems or weaknesses to their strengths, they may identify a quality they can use in charting a different course.

3. "What do you believe I can do to help you? What do you imagine me doing?" This question is more than an attempt to assess their faith in you. It is an opportunity to discover how much they have thought about counseling and what their expectations are. It also gives you an opportunity to sketch for them what you believe about your role and about how change is possible. In short, examining beliefs is important so that each person focuses on his own commitment and behavior rather than complaining about the partner's behavior. This also helps each person examine his role in producing or maintaining the problem. Finally, it places responsibility on the couple to produce a solution or to be amenable to any additional guidance or knowledge you believe would help them.

Teaching Correct Principles

Much of your contribution to solving marriage problems will come from your teaching of correct principles. The reason this chapter addressed attitudes and beliefs first is because the attitudes of a couple toward their own beliefs and commitments is the key to the quality of their marriage. It has already been illustrated that a destructive attitude is itself the biggest obstacle faced by a couple. It has also been shown that if people think their attitudes are not their responsibility, they will continue to suffer needlessly at the hands of their self-selected enemy. Without giving up such a point of view, hostile couples will continue in their hostility. If, after your attempts to teach the Golden Rule, the attitudes of the couple seem unchanged, you may have a couple whose attitude is accurately described by this verse: "For what doth it profit a man if a gift is bestowed upon him, and he receive not the gift? Behold, he rejoices not in that which is given unto him, neither rejoices in him who is the giver of the gift." (D&C 88:33.)

In other words, when your attempt to give the gift of correct principles is resisted, the couple sees neither the value of your counsel nor your commitment as the giver. They see no value in the valuable. However, given the softening of a husband's heart, given the flicker of acknowledgment by a wife that she could be different, formal sharing of principles like compassion, repentance, forgiveness, sacrifice, or commitment can help. Notice that even these fundamentals flow more from the heart than from the head. In teaching these principles, it may be inappropriate to turn the counseling session into a long gospel discourse. On the other hand, a way to link a gospel ideal with the couple's circumstances is to ask them to do it.

You could present a case study from the scriptures, giving the couple the responsibility to interpret it. Or you might simply ask what forgiveness or compassion means to them. Your goal is to link some gospel idea with an illustration or example and with the couple's own experiences. The couple who participates in the pondering and the discovery of the meanings of gospel truths is already taking responsibility to link theory with practice.

The Problem of Ignorance

Not all people seeking counsel in their marriages have problems because of negative attitudes. Sometimes couples may approach you with a sincere and mutual concern about how they are living their lives. Sometimes financial difficulties or physical illness or chronic employment problems are related to their lack of knowledge or wisdom. Where you are knowledgeable in these matters, share your knowledge. Where you can introduce only an idea or two, refer the couple to trusted resource people. Point them in a direction you believe will lead them to be independent of you and give them the chance to become knowledgeable.

When the issue is how to accomplish a task rather than how to solve relationship problems, you can become a source of knowledge to the couple. Because their relationship is not part of the problem, they can use your knowledge to overcome it. When the couple is already united by love, forgiveness, and patience, their resources are ready to be applied to situations where lack of knowledge is the only limitation.

This is another important reason to see the couple together. You then have a cooperative unit that can work on the problem. Often, a problem caused by a lack of knowledge can be addressed most effectively in two ways, from the two different perspectives of the marriage partners themselves.

The Couple Versus Their Circumstances

When couples are united but face challenges that seem overwhelming, it is still important to leave the responsibility for decisions and actions on their shoulders. More than one sincere counselor has been blamed by couples because they "did what the counselor told us to do." Perhaps the following guidelines will help you counsel a couple without taking from them the responsibility:

1. Define the problem or identify the goal.

2. Examine the resources available to solve the problem or reach the goal. These include spiritual, human, and material resources.

3. Discuss and explore how the resources available can be used to solve the problem or move toward the goal.

Obviously, much pondering, information gathering, honest sharing, prayer, and sometimes trial-and-error experiences are part of this seemingly simplistic set of suggestions. Nevertheless, these suggestions provide a structure on which the couple can hang their problems, examine them, and move toward solutions.

What about Sex?

Some difficulties really are the result of ignorance of body functions and the processes of conception and reproduction. In such cases, it may be necessary for the couple to obtain competent written medical information or to consult with a physician.

More often, however, sexual problems are a specific reflection of more general relationship problems. The couple are not physically close because they are not emotionally close (and they may not be emotionally close because they are not spiritually in tune). If a couple refuses to communicate about financial matters or decides to punish each other over conflicting child-rearing practices, then those same refusals and petty attitudes will be brought to their physical relationship. In such cases, sex becomes just another weapon in an emotional war, not a means of blessing and bonding.

If a couple proposes that their problem is sexual, resist the temptation to launch into medical explanations or recommendations. Look for problems of attitude. Ask them to discuss their general relationship. Look for clues of their level of compassion and mutual respect as they discuss anything from their hobbies to how they have decorated their home. If their discussion of such matters is done with warmth and reverence for each other, their sexual problem may be one in which additional knowledge about sexuality is needed. When a couple's feelings are harsh or distant, then an examination, reevaluation, and abandoning of such attitudes is necessary before it will be clear whether there even is a sexual problem. Emotional bonding and oneness is always a prerequisite to quality intimacy.

Seeking Oneness

Ultimately, marriage counseling should help a couple feel as one. The biggest obstacle to that oneness is the couple's refusal to be one. This occurs when they withhold their hearts and refuse to live by their commitments and covenants to one another. Such refusals produce many of the negative attitudes discussed earlier in this chapter.

In a sense, being one is synonymous with the couple's living by the light and truth they have. It means turning to their marriage with full purpose of heart. When couples do this, it is amazing what their resources are and what solutions become obvious. In this oneness, each partner sees that the best interests of one partner truly are the best interests of the other. Not only is it to their mutual advantage to leave behind competitive interests, but the very process of thinking together about their future promotes oneness.

Until a couple gives up the idea that their personal behaviors and goals are more important than their togetherness, they will perpetuate their problems, and they will not be one no matter how much outside intervention there may be. The basic truth is that *the power is in the hands of the couple* to solve their problems.

When Your Efforts Are in Vain

If a man climbing a mountain stops climbing and does not reach the top, the observer may never know the answer to this question: "Did the man stop climbing because he could not go on, or because he would not?" And if, after your own prayerful efforts, the couple does not resolve their difficulties, then, without some prompting of the Spirit, you may never know why.

Whether you failed to teach them or they refused to be

taught does not change the need for you to acknowledge the futility of your visits together. It may be wise, however, to refer the couple elsewhere.

Remember, because "the power is in [them]" to change, if they do change, it is their victory, not yours. And if they do not change, it is their tragedy, not yours, although you will rejoice in their progress or mourn their refusal to change.

In referring a couple, you are suggesting another tool. The following questions will help you decide whether to refer a couple elsewhere:

1. Is there a lack of compassion on your part for the couple?

2. Are the hours this couple will require a just way to spend your time?

3. Is there any evidence of physical violence or of life-threatening behavior in the family?

4. Is it apparent that one member of the couple dislikes you, even after several meetings? (This should be confronted directly, for such an attitude may be given up, but referral may still be the proper course.)

5. Is the way a family member deals with reality bizarre, unpredictable, or dangerous?

6. Is it possible that some medical or other knowledge must be brought to bear on the problem?

7. Is there no progress or change in the couple?

Summary

In marriage counseling, it is important to see the couple together and to assess and discern their general attitude toward one another. This is the crux of most marriage problems. Until negative attitudes are given up, there is little chance of change.

However, as compassionate understanding replaces blaming attitudes, the couple can move toward independence and to solving problems on their own. If the couple does not progress, you may want to refer them to someone else.

SUGGESTED READINGS

Brent A. Barlow, *What Husbands Expect of Wives* (Salt Lake City: Deseret Book Company, 1983).

—————, *What Wives Expect of Husbands* (Salt Lake City: Deseret Book Company, 1982).

Spencer W. Kimball, *Marriage and Divorce* (Salt Lake City: Deseret Book Company, 1976).

C. S. Lewis, *The Great Divorce* (New York: MacMillan Publishing, 1946; pb, 1978).

Neal A. Maxwell, *That My Family Should Partake* (Salt Lake City: Deseret Book Company, 1974).

Terrance D. Olson, "The Compassionate Marriage Partner," *Ensign* 12 (August 1982): 14-17.

A. Lynn Scoresby, *The Marriage Dialogue* (Menlo Park, CA: Addison-Wesley, 1977).

11

Children, Behavior, and Discipline
Suzanne Hanna

This chapter is for adults who are suffering seriously from the chronic misbehavior of a child (ages three to eleven). This chapter is not for those who wish only to correct minor irritations. If you are not engaged in a painful struggle, you will likely read these pages and disagree with what is said or think of other ideas more comfortable for your own situation. This is as it should be, for your problem may not be as severe as those spoken of here. If, however, you have exhausted your resources and feel a need for extra help, this chapter is for you.

What Is Discipline?
Discipline is a word commonly used in connection with child rearing. Often parents ask, "What is the best way to discipline our children?" Sometimes they say, "If you disobey me, I will have to discipline you." We have all heard the phrase "Spare the rod and spoil the child," which is also related to discipline. Basically, we think of discipline as a certain method used to bring about obedience in children. *Webster's New Collegiate Dictionary* gives several definitions of discipline, including these: "Training that corrects, molds, or perfects the mental faculties or moral character; punishment; control gained by enforcing obedience or order."

The last two meanings imply the use of force. The first meaning, however, deals with an educational process. There are crucial differences between discipline through force and discipline through education, and we must be careful in deciding which to apply in a Latter-day Saint home. The most important difference has to do with power. Definitions of power in the secular world are very different from definitions of power and authority in the scriptures. The nations of the world are trying to decide who has the strongest military force, and in many families, individuals are trying desperately to determine who is boss. Both nations and families treat power as the exercise of control and authority. Such exercise also uses force to discipline.

The scriptures reveal a different use of power and authority. In Doctrine and Covenants 121:41-43, we read, "No power or influence can or ought to be maintained by virtue of the priesthood, only by persuasion, by long-suffering, by gentleness and meekness, and by love unfeigned; by kindness, and pure knowledge, which shall greatly enlarge the soul without hypocrisy, and without guile—reproving betimes with sharpness, when moved upon by the Holy Ghost; and then showing forth afterwards an increase of love toward him whom thou hast reproved, lest he esteem thee to be his enemy."

It is evident from these verses that power is the exercise of inner strength. Righteous power enlarges one's soul from the inside, not one's control of people on the outside. In searching the scriptures for information on disciplining children, one finds that the word *discipline* is never used. Instead, the scriptures exhort parents to teach and train their children. (See Deuteronomy 4:10; Proverbs 22:6; D&C 93:40-44.) Therefore, we should regard discipline as an educational process.

Discipline problems may include constant disobedience, uncontrollable anger, disrespect, truancy, withdrawal, lying, stealing, and moodiness. For adults helping children with such problems, the greatest temptation is to respond with secular power instead of spiritual power. Unfortunately, external attempts to control usually only make the problem worse. Therefore we should think of discipline as a process that does not produce immediate results. As Albert Schweitzer has remarked, things take time: "No ray of sunlight is ever lost, but the green which it awakes into existence needs time to sprout, and it is not always granted to the sower to see the harvest. All work that is worth anything is done in faith."

Why is faith needed in child rearing? It is needed to overcome two common misconceptions:

1. *If parents do everything right, children will do everything right.* If this were true, there would have been no war in our premortal existence. Godhood and parenthood involve rising above anger and embarrassment over our children's choices. Our personal righteousness *can* compensate for the loss felt with disobedient children. The compensation comes when we recognize that the family is a stewardship for learning, not a possession for personal gain. We must define righteousness as our own progress toward compatibility. Then we can see a rebellious child as an opportunity to develop greater tolerance for differences. Such tolerance brings the real assurance that "families are forever." Without this tolerance, we may lose not one, but many, because the Lord's children are all unique, free agents.

2. *If the child is misbehaving, he should be the one to change.* This sounds logical, but since adults are the ones who recognize the problem, they should be responsible for the first change. This does *not* mean that parents are to blame for the problem. It means that they have a greater capacity for understanding, so it is up to them to change to invite the child to change.

At this point, you may exclaim, "Surely this does not mean I should sit back, have faith, and do nothing, does it?" Of course not. But gospel-centered discipline is different from what the world expects. Because secular power is accepted in the world, spiritual power will sometimes seem contrary to common sense. "Faith is not to have a perfect knowledge of things." (Alma 32:21.)

Four Steps to Discipline

The following comments are often used to describe children with problems:

"She's so mean and hateful."

"He acts like he doesn't care about anything."

"She can't do anything right."

"He's a smart aleck."

"She's always asking for trouble."

"He likes to put on his helpless act."

"She's so lazy."

"He never listens."

These descriptions are often used by adults who draw their conclusions from the behavior they observe. However, such descriptions fail to solve the underlying problem. Instead of judging the child's behavior, we must first identify his emotional needs. We must reassure him of his worth. Then we must build his confidence. Finally, if misbehavior persists, we must introduce consequences to help the child learn greater responsibility.

Step One: Understand the Child's Emotional Needs

Children with chronic behavior problems generally misbehave for two reasons. First, their sense of security is threatened, and second, they do not recognize their uniqueness. An insecure child is one who believes that his thoughts, feelings, and actions are inferior. Such a child has little hope that anything about himself is really all right. He lacks confidence that his needs are healthy. Such a child sees himself as different and assumes that this difference is bad. He feels unique but does not realize that his uniqueness can help his family. Such a child feels lonely, even though he seems aggressive. His true feelings are often kept inside and are not shown in his behavior until his parents begin to reinterpret what they see. Usually the child's bad behavior drives people away from him when the very thing he needs is closeness to loved ones. This is why it is important for parents to understand their child's feelings and talk with the child about them.

When bad behavior has become a pattern, the original circumstances that led to the behavior are forgotten, but the behavior persists. However, a loving and inquisitive parent can eventually help a child understand his behavior. It is important that the adult remain loving, kind, and curious rather than serious and worried. This reassures the child and builds his security. Here is an example of such a discussion:

Father:	I understand you were sent to the principal's office again today.
Son:	Yeah.
Father:	I'm wondering how that happened.
Son:	I don't know. Miss Snow is always mean to me.
Father:	What did she do?
Son:	She made me stay in from recess. I hate her!
Father:	Why did she do that?
Son:	She said I was talking, but I wasn't!
Father:	Well, maybe you're right, but I'm wondering about something else.
Son:	What?
Father:	I'm wondering if you're like me.
Son:	Huh?
Father:	Your mother says that I talk too much when I get nervous or uncomfortable. Since you don't like Miss Snow, I just wondered if you get nervous around her. Is that possible?
Son:	Dad! I told you I wasn't talking, honest!
Father:	I know this is frustrating to you, but just think about it. It may not seem to you like you talk too much, but maybe you're just nervous around her. We all get nervous, so that's no crime. I'm not trying to blame you, Son. I just want to help you figure out how to stay out of trouble with Miss Snow. Maybe we can talk again after you've thought about it.

Such a discussion lays the groundwork for further understanding between father and son. The child may not agree or understand at first. However, after several conversations over several days' time, the child will usually relax and see that the parent is not trying to judge him. If the parent remains calm, the child may eventually reach a conclusion about the reasons for his behavior, such as "Miss Snow al-

ways asks me questions that I can't answer and I feel dumb."
Other typical conclusions are

"My friends always pick me last."

"I'm the shortest one in the class."

"I'm scared Mom is going to die."

"Billy is always such a know-it-all."

"I wish Dad could come back to live in our house."

"Nobody understands me."

"I don't like it when you and Mom fight."

"I'm sad that Julie left our house."

Even when a child understands his feelings, he may not immediately change his behavior. His parents must continue in faith, remembering the counsel given in Ether 12:6: "And now, I, Moroni, would speak somewhat concerning these things; I would show unto the world that faith is things which are hoped for and not seen; wherefore, dispute not because ye see not, for ye receive no witness until after the trial of your faith."

Step Two: Give Reassurance

Reassurance is vital for a child who is just beginning to learn about his own feelings and needs. Privately, he may think, "Something is wrong with me. I'm hopeless." However, if such thoughts are followed by reassurance, the child may find hope in his abilities and confidence that he has something special to offer.

This reassurance should be offered in at least three ways. First, parents should speak to the child about the importance of human differences. They might give examples of such differences between themselves, among the other children in the family, and among other adults and children. Variety is the order of the universe, and parents should explain that differences are healthy and positive.

Second, parents should give reassurance to the child that he has strengths. Occasionally I will hear a parent say, "But Susie really *is* clumsy. She just doesn't seem to have anything going for her." Sometimes a child will seem to lack positive qualities. In such cases, parents should open their hearts and minds to find positive qualities they have overlooked, for every person *is* a child of God with the potential to become like him. This in itself is a positive quality.

Third, share personal experiences similar to those the child is going through. Many parents fear that sharing their mistakes, fears, and inadequacies will give their children justification for their own misbehavior. But if parents share such things in a spirit of empathy and understanding, their children will receive reassurance as they learn that others have overcome the same emotions with which they currently struggle.

Some parents may not have had such problems when they were young. In such cases, they will have to learn vicariously about their child's feelings. But they can also help the child know that even though his situation is different from theirs, he is not alone in his search for confidence and worth.

Step Three: Build Confidence

Adults can help the child build confidence by asking such questions as: "How can we help you feel better and less afraid?" "What can we do to help you learn better ways of behaving?" "Would you like some help in overcoming your feelings?" Above all, adults should express a desire to help rather than to punish the child. If parents do not continue with patience, the child will incorrectly think that insecurity is a sin rather than a legitimate human struggle. With sufficient patience, parents will communicate the security and confidence they want the child to develop.

Step Four: Establish Consequences

The greatest challenge in establishing consequences is to provide enough structure but not too much. It is important to seek a balance between limits that are firmly established and consistently enforced and those that are general enough to permit children to make their own choices and mistakes. Such a balance will build the child's confidence if his parents offer encouragement as he learns from mistakes.

This fourth step should begin with another conversation

with the child when his emotions are calm. Parents should
explain in a friendly way why his behavior is unacceptable,
how they feel about it, and how it affects others. Even if they
secretly believe that the child should know better, they
should be patient and give him the benefit of the doubt.
When we incorrectly judge misbehavior that comes from
anxiety and insecurity, rather than labeling the emotions
themselves, we likely perpetuate those emotions *and* the
misbehavior. Parents should tell the child that they want to
help him learn and remember what acceptable behavior is.
Parents may teach the need for consequences by explaining
that we remember best when we suffer some consequences
for our own actions. Consider this example:

Mother:	Ann, I notice that you are still having a hard time controlling your temper when we ask you to help with chores.
Daughter:	No, I'm not.
Mother:	Well, last night I remember some trouble when I asked you to straighten the family room.
Daughter:	So?
Mother:	You know the talks we've been having about your temper and the lonely feelings you have?
Daughter:	Yeah.
Mother:	I am wondering how we could help you to be more cooperative even when you're feeling lonely. I know it's hard for you to be at a new school where you don't have friends yet, but I'm also getting frustrated because I need your help in the evening when I come home from work. I'm also afraid that when you and I fight, it just adds to your loneliness. Do you think that happens?
Daughter:	I guess so.
Mother:	What would happen if we made a rule that the family room has to be straightened before dinner? Then I wouldn't have to nag you anymore.
Daughter:	Okay.
Mother:	All right, then. If I promise not to nag, it means you will be served dinner only after you've done your work. Do you understand?
Daughter:	Yeah.

In following up on this conversation, the mother should
have to pay attention only to whether or not Ann has com-

pleted her work before dinner. If she has not, the mother may suggest that Ann not come to the table until her work is done. If Ann's temper should flare at this point, the mother should suggest that Ann go without her dinner as a way of *helping her to remember* what is expected of her. This should be done in a friendly way, even if the child is being un-friendly! The consequences should always be something be-sides adult anger, lectures, or rejection.

Appropriate consequences include situations that tem-porarily prevent the misbehavior, such as restriction of a privilege, or that withhold something that is important to the child. Some children act as though no consequences mat-ter to them. This may puzzle their parents. However, careful consideration will usually reveal certain activities, friends, or privileges that are important and enjoyable to them. Even a withdrawn child, for example, may be required to spend some time with the family in exchange for some privilege they have been taking for granted. If parents are firm and consistent, the child will learn that all things have a price. If parents *remain* positive and firm over *several weeks of great resistance*, they and their child will both learn confidence and move forward together.

Many people think that establishing consequences is just another way to punish a child for doing something wrong. In reality, this depends upon the attitude of the adults.

It is helpful for children to experience a consequence when they have violated the rights of others or disobeyed im-portant rules. If consequences are carried out calmly, the child will learn from it. If punished in anger or disgust, the child will obey because he fears anger, but this fear will over-ride learning.

Some parents wonder, "How do I accept the child with-out making him think I approve of his misbehavior? Parents seem to think that a friendly interaction will lead the child to conclude that the parent approves of his deeds. This conclu-sion is incorrect *if the parent consistently applies the conse-quences of the misbehavior*. Consider the father of the Prodi-gal Son. Because the son had experienced consequences as a natural result of his decisions, the father did not have to punish him in any way. Instead, he greeted him with open arms, as well as with a robe, a ring, and a fatted calf. (See Luke 15:22-23.) Did this father approve of his son's deeds? No. Was the son "getting away with something?" No. The wise father knew that the son had suffered the consequences of his sins. This was sufficient. His method of discipline was not to control but to teach through acts of love. This is spiritual power, the best example we can set for our children.

SUGGESTED READINGS

G. Hugh Allred, *How to Strengthen Your Marriage and Family* (Provo, Utah: Brigham Young University Press, 1976).

Don Dinkmeyer and Gary McKay, *Raising a Responsible Child* (New York: Simon and Schuster, 1973).

Terrance D. Olson, "When Your Children Lie to You," *Ensign* 7 (August 1977): 17-19.

ABOUT THE AUTHOR

Dr. Suzanne Hanna received her bachelor's degree from Brigham Young University, her master's degree from the University of Utah, and her Ph.D. from BYU. A marriage and family therapist in private practice, Dr. Hanna has taught in the BYU Department of Family Sciences and has been a psychotherapist in the Mental Health Center at LDS Hospital in Salt Lake City.

In the Church, Dr. Hanna has served in many capacities, including as a Sunday School teacher, a Relief Society teacher, a Young Women's adviser, and a member of a stake Relief Society board.

She lives in Madison, Wisconsin.

12

Adolescence
C. Richard Chidester

Adolescence is the period when young people undergo radical changes in physiology, attitudes, and social relationships as they grow from childhood to adulthood. Adolescence begins when puberty sets in and ends in the early twenties when the person is reasonably independent from his parents.

Adolescence is primarily limited to industrially advanced societies, because these societies require highly specialized patterns of behavior and skills not required in less advanced societies. In these advanced societies, marriage and economic independence are usually delayed. The complex preparation required for adulthood leads to much of the adolescent turmoil observed in industrial nations. However, the belief in Western societies that conflicts between parents and children automatically intensify during adolescence has been greatly exaggerated. Family ties remain strong during adolescence, and most adolescents adopt, rather than reject, their parents' values.

For the adolescent, much is happening all at once. Physically, he has a period of accelerated growth second only to the first two years of life. Physical development brings changes in self-concept. Psychologically, he embarks on the challenge of becoming independent and of establishing his own identity. He also learns many of his capabilities and limitations.

While trying to answer the questions of who and what he

is, the adolescent must learn to establish close relationships with others, particularly those of the opposite sex outside his family. This should be a gradual process so that he can understand his new emotions. This is one reason the Church encourages teenagers to wait until they are sixteen to date. By that time, they are more mature in the way they manage their feelings.

The changing emotions of adolescents is associated with rapid changes in their physiology. Heightened emotionality may be marked by a low tolerance for frustration, or by quarrelsomeness. Knowing this, adults should not overreact to teenage "moods," which can range from hysteria at a basketball game to total depression right afterward because a "special someone" did not notice them.

Adolescents sometimes withhold information from those in authority to protect themselves. That is why, if you want personal information from them, you have to ask for it. They will seldom reveal themselves. They sense that the more adults know about how they think and feel, the more influence adults can have over them. For example, the more adults know how strongly teenagers want to drive, the more the adults may be tempted to use driving privileges to manipulate teens into doing what the adults want. Parents need to understand this reluctance to talk. It is not from lack of love and esteem.

Adolescents are often susceptible to the influences of peers and of people they idealize, people who can interpret their feelings for them or interpret what is happening to them. Music frequently expresses feelings they can't understand or otherwise explain. Adolescents often use information from peers to help them create an identity that differentiates them from their parents. As they explore various roles and life-styles, they become aware of and sensitive to others who give them responses about their behavior.

The adolescent's self-concept, his perception of his body, attitudes, thoughts, emotions, and behavior, is fluctuating. New expectations, sexual feelings, and behavioral challenges are used by young people to redefine their self-concepts, modify their attitudes, and test previously held values in light of their changed circumstances.

With maturity, the adolescent's need to identify with others diminishes, and his own ideas and values provide the framework for his identity. Since self-esteem or feelings of worth partially stem from daily social experiences, adolescents need encouragement, support, and approval. Although our culture promotes the idea that peer pressures and family commitments are opposing forces, the family can actually provide a foundation for a teenager's success in the world outside the family.

Problems Related to Adolescence

Family conflicts often occur because adolescents must learn the relationship between freedom and authority. Conflicts typically occur when parents overreact to behavior that is actually quite normal. Part of the problem is that parents want to spare their children the anxieties they experienced as teenagers. Usually, however, adolescents cannot avoid such experiences.

Control is generally thought to be the central issue in the "letting go" process between parents and teens: *what* are the rules or limits and *who* gets to set them? The adolescent naturally wants more and more control over his life—more freedom to decide things for himself. Parents, on the other hand, often feel it is their responsibility to draw the line, even when the teenager thinks that this is imposing unfair demands.

The teenager may see his parents' help as interference, their genuine concern as babying, and their advice as bossing. Parents may find themselves puzzled about how to help when their guidance is resented and rejected. The natural course when an adolescent rebels or deviates from the rules is to increase parental control. But such control usually promotes further resistance. By imposing more control, parents may create—or at least encourage—the very behavior they don't want. The result is a power struggle over who is going to control whom. If parents mistakenly think that the issue is really *control*, then the power struggle will continue.

What should parents do? I'm convinced that having a change of heart toward our teens is infinitely more important than learning techniques and skills. This means, first of all, that parents must give up their controlling attitudes, and secondly, that they see themselves as teachers. Often, our attitudes toward teenagers represent an unfair accusation of them. We already accuse them of behaviors or attitudes they do not have. When we try to control them, we have accused them of being the kind of kids who cannot be responsible— they can only be "controlled."

Seeing teenagers as capable of taking responsibility is an attitude that suggests we can teach them responsible living. When parents teach, they are taking responsibility. When parents blame teenagers or circumstances for problems, their attitudes—their hearts—are not right. When their hearts are right and they perceive others compassionately, parents can influence their teens for good and create a better life for all their family members.

So a parent is to be compassionate and teach. What are they to teach? The gospel teaches that even though our environments have powerful influences on us, we are still free to choose whether or not we will allow external forces to control our behavior. Our behavior is not so much a product of what *happens* to us as it is a product of what we *do* with what happens. How we perceive or interpret events suggests our actions. Teenagers deserve to be taught that they are not pushed around by forces beyond their control. Responsible living is possible. Parents who are compassionate teachers do not indulge or excuse teens, but act however love requires, whether firmly or forgivingly.

In one family I was counseling, a sixteen-year-old boy was crude, irresponsible, and unresponsive to parents. He continually provoked his brothers and sisters because he thought they deserved what he did to them.

One Saturday morning he brought a girlfriend home. His mother, being more concerned about the curlers in her hair than her son or the girl, greeted the girl tersely and then quickly excused herself because she felt embarrassed about her appearance. After the son took the girl home, he came back and verbally attacked his mother for being so rude and insensitive to his girlfriend. As the mother listened to her son, she did not try to justify or defend herself. She realized he was right. When he finished, she said, "You're right, son. I was insensitive. I'll bet your girlfriend thought I didn't approve of her by the way I acted. I'm sorry for acting this way. I was just thinking of myself rather than being concerned about your feelings." Her honest response softened his heart and he began to confide in her.

This example allows us to see that we, by our attitudes, promote a certain amount of adolescent resistance. Rebellion is not necessarily the fault of the parents, nor should parents passively tolerate it. But compassion is essential if teenage belligerence is to be met successfully. Compassionate parents can bring their children back to them.

The following patterns tend to show up in families where there is little compassion and where family members see each other as irritants: the parent will not take the adolescent's views and opinions into account; he will frequently interrupt the adolescent; he will not follow the adolescent's suggestions; and he will interrogate the adolescent. Seeing such patterns, the adolescent often concludes that he isn't worth much. He may feel extreme anger and rage, which can lead to deviant behavior.

As an adolescent begins to provoke others and to strike out, his parents' negative feelings toward their child are confirmed. This is collusion, mutual blaming between parent and child. The seeds of adolescent problems are often sown in the elementary years—before actual conflicts begin—because parents and children have been harboring negative attitudes toward each other. Parents get what they give. They reap what they sow.

What the Counselor Should and Should Not Do

The counselor's goal is to help change attitudes and perceptions of parents and adolescents, thus changing their behavior. To focus on outward behavior without changing the heart is to hack at the leaves and not at the roots. For "out of the abundance of the heart [the] mouth speaketh." (Luke 6:45.)

For people's hearts to change, people must acknowledge that other people and circumstances do not cause their problems. Our behavior is a product of our own way of seeing the world. If we see ourselves and the world accusingly, fearfully, or defensively, we will interpret the feedback we get in a way that justifies those perceptions. "As [a man] thinketh in his heart, so is he." (Proverbs 23:7.) Therefore, a counselor might help both parent and child to understand that it is not the other's behavior that is causing their hurt, anger, or resentment, but their own taking offense at the other's behavior.

It is self-deception to believe that our negative feelings and behavior are caused by others or by our circumstances. Our children may behave unseemly, but when we are angry with them, we are behaving just as unseemly. If we perceive them as the reason we can't help our feelings, we are blind to the truth, and the truth cannot be in us. (See 1 John 1:6-10.) Specifically, you as a counselor could

1. *Help both parents and children to see the need to take responsibility for their own behavior.* Help both to be honest about their own problems and to stop worrying about what is wrong with the other person. If you can help them see each other honestly and compassionately, their hearts will soften and they will automatically begin to communicate more cooperatively and effectively.

2. *Teach parents about the nature of adolescence.* They need to understand what adolescents face in developing mature thoughts, feelings, and actions.

3. *Establish a relationship with the adolescent by spending time alone with him. Without this, you may be perceived as another authority figure who is siding with the parents.*

In your own words, reflect back to the adolescent his feelings and opinions as he expresses them. In this way he can know you understand how he feels. This does not mean you necessarily agree with him, but that you understand how he feels.

4. *Help parents gradually give more responsibility to the adolescent.* In the early years of marriage, parents naturally have control of their children, but adolescents want to be treated as equals and want to negotiate for "control." Parents and children can never be complete equals in all areas. But there are certain responsibilities in which everyone must share and cooperate, and there are rules about how people should treat each other that apply to everyone in the family, including parents.

It is also important to remember that adolescents want to be governed more by implicit rules than explicit ones. Small children want explicit rules like "Please cut the lawn right now," while adolescents want to hear "Please get the lawn cut today." The latter allows the budding adult to decide when and how the lawn will get cut and makes him feel responsible, capable, and free to decide.

5. *Avoid a negative triangle.* Two parents and an adolescent form a triangle, and that triangle often ends up with two parents in a coalition against the child. To have a healthy triangle, each person must work on his relationship with the other two individually and then help the other two have a good relationship as well. In a healthy triangle, communication is open and decisions are made mutually. Family gossip, in which the sins of a child are rehearsed in the child's absence, can be a way of seeing the child uncompassionately. We should confront directly those we love.

6. *Encourage tolerance for differences of opinion.* If adolescents can't achieve separateness by having opinions of their own, they sometimes take the wrong road to separateness by rejecting their parents and turning to self-destructive behavior such as drugs, alcohol, sex, and deviant behavior to hurt or destroy their parents. What they don't understand is that when they reject the values of their parents, they reject their own internal system as well. Most teens identify so

strongly with their parents that when they act in antisocial ways they actually hurt themselves more than they hurt their parents. In healthy families, children can be themselves without being rejected or ridiculed. Being tolerant of differences of opinion is not the same as "giving in."

7. *Teach parents to be true to themselves.* If parents are true to themselves, the adolescent will probably feel good about them and respect them. Parents should allow the adolescent to be true to himself without provoking him to feel ashamed for disagreeing or feeling differently. The key is to be honest without accusing.

Parents might try statements like this: "I really want you to serve a mission, and so does the Lord. But the decision is up to you. I will love you no matter what you do." Such an approach gives the adolescent the firm guidance he needs but also allows him room to make his own choices. But parents must not use such a statement to manipulate their child. Sincerity is essential. Adolescents easily detect phoniness.

8. *Foster high levels of trust, cohesion, and openness.* Trust comes from being able to predict that others in the family will usually act in a warm, caring way. If the child puts his arm around his parent, he trusts his parent; he's not afraid of him. Cohesion comes from sharing feelings and experiences. Openness is the freedom to express feelings about things. Family activities and traditions help create cohesion and openness. Adolescents frequently have a hard time expressing emotions. But in families that lack freedom of expression, it is particularly difficult.

9. *Avoid siding with the parents against the child or vice versa.* Help both sides to be open, honest, just, and unaccusing, and to seek the Spirit as their greatest aid in changing their hearts and attitudes. This will help them create a healthy relationship and avoid turning each other into enemies.

10. *Help the parents and the adolescent to see that it is not so much what they need to begin doing that will bring about the improvements they desire, but what they need to undo or stop doing.* The Lord said to say nothing but repentance unto

this generation (D&C 11:9), and repentance means to stop doing things that are wrong. The parents and teenager need to stop perceiving accusingly, to stop provoking and becoming provoked by taking offense, and to stop shifting the responsibility for their feelings onto each other or their circumstances.

11. *Teach parents to let their adolescents express themselves.* Adolescents are struggling to move from being externally controlled to being self-directed. As parents help them identify what they want to do or want the parents to do, adolescents learn to take responsibility for their actions and don't simply react against "shoulds" and "oughts." Questions like "What do you think about . . . ?" "How do you feel about . . . ?" and "How do you want to handle that?" help them share in the control and, at the same time, help them learn to make responsible decisions.

12. *Teach parents to give legitimate praise.* Because adolescents sometimes feel awkward, rejected, or confused, they suffer from what might be termed "approval anxiety." Teenagers, like younger children, need all of the support and legitimate praise we can give. They may act as if they don't need approval or affection from adults. Sometimes they might feel that parents are using their love to control them. But they will accept affection if the total relationship is good.

It is important to be sensitive in praising a teenager. Praise can imply judgment of personality and character if it isn't genuine and couched in descriptive terms. For example, if a daughter cleans the kitchen well, her mother might say, "Thank you very much for cleaning the kitchen. It really made my day." That is honest praise that describes what was done.

13. *Teach parents how to encourage their teenagers appropriately.* Parents need to be willing to remind and encourage without being offensive. If an adolescent repeatedly forgets or simply fails to follow through on his responsibilities, parents must be willing to remind him with considerateness and courtesy. This process may seem endless and unrewarding, but it is often normal and necessary. Parents can

do it effectively only when they perceive their adolescents realistically and compassionately. Little wonder the scriptures mention patience and long-suffering so frequently!

14. *Encourage parents to take time to talk to their adolescents.* It can be very meaningful to adolescents for parents to give him their time and attention without his having to ask for it. At such times they may want to share with him what they experienced when they were teenagers, what is happening to them in the present, how they feel, or what they like and don't like.

Unfortunately, parents tend to interact less and less with their children as they get older. Just the opposite should be true. Adolescents thrive on self-disclosure by their parents as long as it doesn't degenerate into moralizing about the good old days or to telling them how they should feel.

This is also the most important time for parents to talk about physical development and to disclose their own concerns about the moral code as they grew up. If they don't teach their children the world will. Parents must teach them the sacredness of their sexual capacities as an alternative to the carnality the world is promoting.

15. *Teach parents how to express unconditional love.* No behavior technique can take the place of communicating unconditional love to children. Conditional love tells them they are loved only if and when they do certain things that please the parents. But unconditional love means loving them as they are, with no strings attached.

Two LDS boys became addicted to drugs and decided to leave home to be on their own. The parents of one said, "If you move out, don't ever come back until you quit your filthy habit." The other boy's parents said, "You may move out if you wish, but you may return at any time. We love you, and there's nothing you can do to destroy that love. Remember, you'll always be welcome in our home."

Even such unconditional love does not always ensure that the problem will be solved, but in this instance the second boy eventually served a mission because of the influence of his parents' unconditional love. Maintaining their relationship with their son was more important to them than proving that they had control over him.

16. *Teach parents to be a step ahead of adolescent problems by trying new things.* Hiking, taking trips, and doing things to expand the teenager's awareness help build the parent-child relationship. That is what adolescents are after during this transition time of their life. This should be done over again with every adolescent in the family.

Consider the following quotation from Amiel's Journal. It was actually written in 1853, more than a century ago:

> Self-government with tenderness—there you have the condition of all authority over children. The child must discover in us no passion, no weakness of which he can make use; he must feel himself powerless to deceive or to trouble us; then he will recognize in us his natural superiors, and he will attach a special value on our kindness, because he will respect it. The child who can rouse in us anger, or impatience, or excitement, feels himself stronger than we, and a child only respects strength. . . . This is why the first principle of education is: train yourself, and the first rule to follow if you wish to possess yourself of a child's will is: master your own.

A Final Word of Advice

You, the counselor, may have to spend time alone with the parents in order to help *them* become united before counseling with the family together or with them and their problem teenager. Relating well to teenagers requires a loving unity between parents so they can arrive at agreement about their children and support each other. If parents do not agree with each other, dealing with adolescent development can become a real crisis and can make unresolved differences between parents worse. On the other hand, unity between parents encourages family unity.

The counselor must be flexible in his approach because he may want to spend time with the parents alone, the children alone, the whole family together, or with the adolescent alone at various times to bring about the desired results. It is also helpful at times to bring in members of the extended family, such as grandparents, in order to resolve certain conflicts. It may also be necessary to reach out to teachers, school administrators, or others outside the family to properly understand the problems involved or to work out solutions.

SUGGESTED READINGS

A. Bandura, "The Stormy Decade: Fact or Fiction?" *Psychology in the Schools.* 1 (1964):224-31.

Haim G. Ginott, *Between Parent and Teenager* (New York: Avon Books, 1971).

Robert E. Grindler, *Adolescence* (New York: John Wiley, 1973).

M. Powell, *The Psychology of Adolescence,* 2nd ed. (Indianapolis: Bobbs-Merrill, 1971).

ABOUT THE AUTHOR

Dr. C. Richard Chidester received his bachelor's degree from the University of Utah, followed by master's and Ph.D. degrees from Brigham Young University. Presently he works in the Church Education System as associate area director for the Davis County (Utah) seminaries. He is also a licensed practicing marriage and family counselor. He has taught at BYU and at the LDS institutes of religion at the University of Utah and Weber State College.

Dr. Chidester is a popular and inspirational speaker. He is widely known throughout the Church for his contributions to BYU Campus Education Week and other Continuing Education programs.

Dr. Chidester has served as a member of an instructional development committee of the Church. He has also served as a bishop, a counselor in a bishopric, and a high councilor.

He and his wife, Kathryn, are the parents of seven children.

13
After Divorce
Jane Beuhring

The emergency-room door opens and paramedics rush in with a seriously injured person. Being more accustomed to physical pain and suffering than most of us, the hospital personnel seem to function automatically, almost unemotionally. They monitor vital signs, introduce life-saving procedures, and pursue a systematic evaluation of injuries.

Unlike the emotionally seasoned workers in the emergency room, lay counselors have often not been exposed to enough emotional tragedies to withstand becoming emotionally involved themselves. Because of their emotional involvement, they may be somewhat ineffective.

It is essential to clean the wound before it can heal, yet we're apprehensive about inflicting more pain. Because it is not pleasant to share others' emotional pain, we may find ourselves applying small, convenient bandages when we should be performing major surgery. So it is with the emotionally distressed divorcée or the person about to be divorced. The healing process is often long, complex, and painful.

As a counselor in the Church, you are in a position to give spiritual as well as temporal guidance. Both should be given with an eternal perspective.

The experiences through which the divorced person has passed are much like hands molding potter's clay. The person's responses to your counsel may be soft, pliable, willing, and submissive, or bitter, hard, and dry, like unyielding clay—resistant to change.

The apparently hardened person may feel alienated and may alienate others. But beneath the hard exterior you may find a person crying out for acceptance and love. This facade is a poor protection against pain; it usually invites responses that are just the opposite of what the person hopes to receive in return. This hard exterior may be characterized by defensive, angry, or justifying behavior and responses. When someone feels attacked and challenged by life, it is unlikely that he will see that it is possible to give up his negative feelings.

Pain is often a necessary part of change, and can be a very useful tool when the results are productive. However, people often resist when we try to force them to give up their pain. Usually the person is unaware that he is holding on to pain so desperately. It may be true that he has been wronged, unjustly dealt with, and persecuted; nevertheless, until he is truly willing to put all that behind him, he is savoring the pain.

It is up to you to show love, acceptance, and concern for the person without sanctioning his anger. When given sincere love and concern, the person can become soft and pliable—capable of being molded anew.

Someone has said that if you give a man food, you feed him for a day, but if you can teach him how to grow his food, he can feed himself for life. The divorced person may feel a hunger, but not know what will be nourishing. The food you have to give is "every word that proceedeth forth from the mouth of God." This food, this truth, does not exist just for a select group; it exists for all. Obedience to the basic truths of the gospel is necessary for a person to find happiness, and the divorced person is no exception. The person may say, "Oh, what do you know about divorce?" or "You've never been through what I have." This is unimportant. The real question the person faces is not "How can he understand me?" but "What am I to understand?" Or more significantly, not "What should I do?" but "What should I be?" When "What should I be?" is answered in an eternal perspective—I should be forgiving, charitable, industrious, self-reliant, and so on—then the answer to "What should I do?" may come clearly into focus.

Too often we resist doing what we know is right because we see ourselves as helpless to affect circumstances and powerless to create change. This sense of powerlessness, helplessness, and lack of self-esteem can be the result not only of divorce, but of the circumstances leading to divorce.

The Single Adult

Those divorcing who have no children may have a different set of concerns than do divorcing parents. The childless divorcée may be more isolated. Of course, they do have relationships with their parents, siblings, cousins, and so on, but the couple friends they had while married may no longer be interested in bowling or dinners together—even if the divorced person brings a date. For a person to be *labeled* as divorced, by ward members or others, is unfortunate. The divorced person is still a *person* with inherent worth.

The Emotions of the Divorced

The emotions of those who lose a marriage partner through divorce are similar to the feelings of those who lose a spouse through death. These feelings are discussed by Elisabeth Kübler-Ross in her book *On Death and Dying*. These feelings or stages are *denial, anger, bargaining, depression*, and *acceptance*.[1]

The first stage, *denial*, helps buffer the shock of divorce. It is a temporary defense against the unwanted or unexpected. It allows the person to adjust at his own speed.

Anger is the second stage. It may be vented in all directions. Bitterness, anger, and resentment, whether against the person's former spouse, his circumstances, society, or the Lord, are extremely destructive. These feelings may greatly hinder the person's progress. One is not ready or even able to love again until he abandons these feelings. Negative emotions do far more damage to those who have them than to the people to whom they are directed.

Bargaining is the third stage of emotional adjustment. Bargaining with the Lord seems to be particularly common among those facing divorce. We all seek answers to our prayers, but the single person often finds himself being obedient to the Lord's commandments in order to receive a specific blessing—namely, a mate. Often, when this blessing does not come, the person becomes angry with the Lord: "I'm being obedient; why does he refuse to bless me?" Such people don't understand two fundamental ideas: (1) that true obedience is submitting to the will of the Lord unconditionally, without selfish motives; (2) the Lord's timetable is not the same as our own. These people need to be encouraged to reexamine their motives for obedience. Are they obedient with their hearts or only as a way to earn blessings?

After one has experienced denial, anger, bargaining, and still their circumstances remain unchanged, he often falls into a state of *depression*, the fourth stage. From this feeling of hopelessness that nothing the person can do will change his relationship with his ex-spouse, a sense of reality and finality may emerge. This prepares the way for *acceptance* of the divorce, the fifth stage. When such acceptance finally occurs, the person will actually be relieved, and peace, direction, and even joy can return to their lives. They are then prepared to build another meaningful relationship. If such a relationship is considered prior to this acceptance, they are not as likely to succeed in it.

Some people will take years to go through these stages. Others will have gone through them before the actual divorce occurs. Some may progress steadily through the cycle, while others will repeatedly regress. If the divorced person is aware that his feelings have also been experienced by others and that he, too, can reach acceptance, he will be somewhat reassured. Acceptance is also something to strive for, for with it comes peace of mind.

Other Feelings of the Divorced

The divorced have the problem of facing family and friends to explain what may be perceived as a failure. Divorce frequently includes feelings of embarrassment and humiliation. The question of mere survival is often overwhelming. The person wonders, "How will I provide for my children and pay the expenses ahead? How well will the children adjust? Where will I work if I have to work? Will people accept me and the children? Will new Church leaders understand? Will I ever be given a trusted position again?" These and many other questions can create negative feelings that need to be understood. Some of these are discussed below.

Low Self-Esteem

The end of an intimate relationship is often accompanied by feelings of low self-esteem. When a person is suffering from low self-esteem, his capacity to function well in society is severely hampered. Communication and problem-solving skills become limited, which causes more problems, which further lower self-esteem. Because feelings of worthlessness are not of God, people with these feelings may not feel comfortable about their relationship with God. Consequently, they may eventually withdraw from the Lord and the Church if they do not receive help.

Guilt and Shame

Even though feelings of guilt and shame are a necessary part of repentance, unnecessary guilt and shame are sometimes experienced by those who have not transgressed but who have divorced. Society may sometimes demand repentance of people from whom no repentance is required. Such feelings in a ward or neighborhood are destructive and counter to gospel teachings. In such a setting, the divorced person may feel so uncomfortable that he becomes inactive, or, if he continues activity in the Church, he may interpret innocent responses as evidence of condemnation.

Helping the Emotionally Troubled

When working with a person who is highly emotional, be cautious in your show of empathy. Yes, your concern needs to be genuine, but if you are not careful, you may end up en-

couraging or reinforcing behavior that may promote dependence on you. Listen for statements by the divorced person
that reflect mature, rational judgment, and reinforce such
statements, encouraging continued good judgment in future
decisions. For example, a divorced woman may come to you
and spend half an hour vacillating between tears and anger.
She may discuss financial, social, emotional, personal, practical, family, and religious concerns. After wearing herself
out emotionally, she may simply stop and say something
like, "Well, this isn't getting me anywhere. I just need to take
things one at a time."

At this point you might say something like, "I can see that
even though you have a number of concerns, you are realistic
enough to see that you can only do so much. And you really
do have the ability to pull yourself together. I'm proud of you
for your ability to be so strong." Whatever you say, be certain
that you are sincere and believe it yourself. No one likes to be
patronized. Even a few comments of support and encouragement are helpful.

It may be that the divorced person is so discouraged that
you may need to point out his personal strengths. You may
say something like, "I know you love your children and are
doing all you can to be a good parent" or "I know you want to
do what's right, and that takes a lot of courage."

Emotions are difficult to deal with at times, but they can
be used to good advantage, for a change in behavior is more
likely to occur when strong emotion is present. However,
what the emotion is may influence whether the change is
good or bad. The divorced person may need to be made
aware of the destructive nature of some emotions, such as
hatred or envy, and rid themselves of them. On the other
hand, feelings of discouragement and frustration may drive
the person to "try anything" to improve his situation.

Concerns of the Divorced

Besides dealing with their emotions, divorced people
have many "practical" concerns. The most common of these
are discussed below.

Telling the Children

Before a divorce, many children begin to feel as if they are no longer loved because their parents are so busy with their marital problems. When the actual divorce occurs, many feel as if they are in some way to blame. They may reprimand themselves and feel sorry for not having been more "obedient." Some may even express this to their parents, begging them to stay together with a promise to "be good."

Most children suspect a divorce is coming before it actually occurs. Many may have lived with the threat for years, and either don't believe it will ever happen or are not surprised by it.

The counselor needs to understand the possible frame of mind of the children of divorced parents—or of those about to be divorced. Parents are often completely unaware that their children feel guilty about the divorce. Consequently, your counsel to the parents might be for them to continually reassure their children of their love for them. The children should never be made to feel that they were in any way responsible for the divorce.

Children may go through the same stages of loss as their parents. If parents are aware of this, they can better help their children adjust.

Breaking the News to Those Outside the Family

One of the first things the newly divorced person has to face is breaking the news to neighbors, friends, business associates, and loved ones. He is sure to get different responses. Many people immediately ask, "Why?" The temptation to respond is great, but trying to explain may prove frustrating and demeaning.

One woman said, "I wanted to tell all. I wanted to be understood and appreciated for the sincere efforts I had made to save the marriage. I wanted people to know I didn't just quit on a whim. It wasn't that the grass looked greener elsewhere; I just knew that it was what I had to do. Where to begin? It began so far back that it's hard to pinpoint exactly. So many destructive events. People wouldn't believe me even if I told them. And even if they did believe me, they would wonder what was wrong with me. Oh, now I sound like a martyr . . . or a saint. I guess it's just easier not to respond at all."

Generally, it appears that the best counsel to give the divorced is to tell as little as possible about the details of the divorce. They need to be prepared for the fact that some may reflect shock, dismay, and, especially with loved ones, hurt and even anger.

A brief statement of fact is usually the easiest for everyone. One woman said that when people asked about her divorce, she would reply, "Oh, didn't you know?" This seemed to limit the request for more details.

It would be ideal if both spouses could mutually agree to keep the details of their divorce private. Unfortunately, many feel so much hurt and bitterness that they cannot resist the opportunity to gain a sympathetic ear.

Even though the divorced need to be encouraged to limit those in whom they confide, they should still be encouraged to find someone that they trust to talk with. Sometimes the best therapy is to be able to talk without being concerned about being judged.

Finances

Having adequate financial resources to provide for themselves and their children is often one of the greatest concerns of the divorced person. This is more often a problem if the mother has custody of the children. Few women are able to earn an income large enough to completely provide for a family. And a relatively small percentage of divorced fathers maintain regular child-support payments.

If income is reduced dramatically, a reevaluation of financial priorities is in order. Often what the person once considered a necessity must now be viewed as a luxury. How well the person's limited resources are managed will greatly determine the financial direction of the family. Poverty is an attitude, not a result of one's economic level. Again, the goal is to teach, not to take over.

Role Models for Children

Too many great men and women have been raised by one parent to attach undue concern to the absolute need for a role model, but providing appropriate role models seems to be a genuine concern to most single parents. Since most children are in the custody of their mother, this concern seems to be most critical in raising boys—particularly in teaching about priesthood responsibilities, sexuality, and preparation for an occupation. Home teachers, Church leaders, and friends can help.

One woman was grateful for a neighbor who frequently called her son over to help with various projects. Even though his "help" may have consisted simply of holding a wrench or bracing an already secure wall, he was sharing time with a man. He may not have actually learned much, but the time spent was reinforcing for the child and reassuring to the mother.

Mothers and fathers as single parents should be encouraged to model their roles to the best of their ability. Mothers should be good homemakers, students of the gospel, and examples of womanliness. Fathers should be good providers and priesthood holders. Children of the same sex will learn their role, as well as children of the opposite sex, if the parent is constant rather than switching roles according to the sex of the child or the occasion. Generally, children learn at least as much about their roles from the parent of the opposite sex as from the parent of the same sex.

Visitation and the "Lollypop War"

Often, the separated parent will frequently visit the children or have them stay over for a weekend. Usually one parent is more financially secure and will try not only to win the children's love with entertainment and gifts but will use these things to "show up" the other parent. This inevitably produces resentment and varying forms of competition between the parents, with the children caught in the middle. This may result in guilt for the less financially secure parent who can't provide as well for the children.

A typical pattern, if such competition is avoided, is for the visits to become less frequent and the gifts less extravagant. Eventually, the visits may stop completely since the motivation to "win" and "get even" decreases and other interests take over.

Good counsel would be for the person to remain true to eternal goals and to have the faith and confidence that the children will recognize truth.

The Parent without Custody

"I miss my kids terribly. When I have them with me, I just can't seem to do enough to show them how much they mean to me. We usually spend our time together doing fun things like going to the zoo, the movies, or the park. We eat out and buy lots of treats and usually a toy or two.

"At first it was fun. It seemed like the only way to let them know I still love them. Now they seem to expect it, even demand it. I've become just the "candy man" to them. What a hollow feeling! All I want to do is be their dad—to tuck them in at night, help with their homework, play catch, and bandage scratched knees."

This example may not reflect the feelings of every parent without custody of their children. Some may be relieved to no longer bear the burden of responsibility. But they are not likely to be the parents you will be counseling.

Too often we think of the divorced parent without the children as "having a free ride," with no commitments, just "foot-loose and fancy free." Little do we consider the pain they may be experiencing. It might help them to suggest ways they can get closer to their children: scouting projects, low-cost entertainment, picnics, camping. The parent needs to keep in mind what is best for his children rather than just what is easiest for him.

Too often the easiest activity is the one that is selected—movies, television, and so on. Not only do the children begin to expect this, but they may become increasingly dissatisfied with the custodial parent, who may not have as many financial resources to entertain them. In such cases, the visiting parent may become just the "candy man," and the custodial parent ends up with dissatisfied children. Such cases are bad for the children as well, because neither parent is attending to what would really be best for children—the parents are only trying to see which of them can be most popular.

Moving

When divorce occurs, obviously one or possibly both parties are forced to move. Whenever possible, especially for the parent with custody of the children, the family should change as few things as possible. They should minimize the number of adjustments necessary and maximize the benefits of the already-established resources and support systems of family, friends, and neighbors.

Still, sometimes it appears easier to "get away and get a fresh start." If divorced people seem determined to move, it may be advisable to explore their motives. If they are running away from problems only to meet those same problems in the new location, you may want to counsel them about solving their problems before they leave. If they are embarrassed or discouraged, they can deal with their feelings more easily in an existing support group than in a brand new one.

When moves do occur, you may want to suggest these things divorced people can do in the new area:

1. Be the first to take a plate of cookies to the immediate neighbors. They shouldn't wait for others to come to them.

2. Introduce themselves to the parents of their children's new friends.

3. Allow those people who feel uncomfortable around divorced people to keep their distance until they are ready to accept the divorced family.

4. Be friendly . . . and patient.

Here are some ways to help divorced people who move into your area:

1. Whenever possible, help the person move.

2. Briefly orient them to your area. Tell them the location of schools, shopping centers, and medical facilities. Tell them your church schedule.

3. Introduce them to others you think they would relate to.

4. Invite them to your home. They will then know at least one family who accepts them.

Whether you are preparing someone to make a successful move or you are receiving someone into your area, your influence may well determine the direction their life will take.

Education

Education is a short-term sacrifice but a long-term gain. Divorced people often think something like this: "How am I going to provide for myself and my children with the skills I have? I'd love to go to college or a trade school, but that's impossible. I just don't have the money."

Too often people give up without even trying. There are many stories of people who have accomplished what they wanted to do in spite of serious obstacles.

One sister had a job as a secretary. The pay was minimal and her interests were elsewhere. She decided to take classes one at a time to complete her education. Upon getting her bachelor's degree, she realized it was not marketable in the real world. Determined to not be a secretary the rest of her life, she applied to a graduate school. She didn't know where the money would come from to go, but felt sure that she should pursue her education. She moved forward one small step at a time, not knowing beforehand how she would accomplish her goal. Eventually she did receive the education—and the job—she desired.

Many resources are available to assist those who are determined to receive an education and have a genuine need to do so—assistantships, scholarships, grants, and school loans.

You may want to consider these questions when counseling a divorced person who needs further education:

1. What training does the person already have?
2. What is needed to obtain further training?
3. What resources are available in the family?

4. What resources are available in the community, the school, and the Church?

5. How willing is the person to make a short-term sacrifice for a long-term gain?

6. How willing is the person to take one step into the dark, by faith, knowing a way will be opened up?

Social and Emotional Needs

Too often the divorced person thinks that the best answer to the problems of divorce is to remarry as soon as possible. He may say, "I have a responsibility to find another partner for my children." Even though this is a worthy goal, it is critical to keep priorities in order. The person should work on having a good relationship with himself, his children, and the Lord. Then he will be in a better position to develop a new marriage relationship. This does not mean the person should have no social contact, but simply that he should exercise caution before vigorously seeking a new spouse. A worthwhile pursuit may be to become the kind of person he himself hopes to find.

Staying Active in the Church

The Church is for *all* people—old, young, rich, poor, married, single, divorced, or widowed. The gospel teaches the necessity of the family for exaltation. But just because one does not currently enjoy the blessings of a complete family is no reason for him to reject ever having one or to envy those who do. The real challenge is to enjoy the total program of the Church *without* having the ideal family situation. One sister was quite inactive while married, but upon obtaining a divorce, she began having family prayer, scripture study, and family home evening. She worked with her children on welfare projects and invited friends in to take cookies to a neighbor. She even set up a limited family preparedness program with each child being responsible for a specific area. She saw the single adult program of the Church as a supplement to rather than a substitute for the Church. Her bishop wisely provided her with a calling that allowed

her maximum time with her children and yet helped her feel
that she was contributing to the ward in a meaningful way.
When home teachers were assigned, she took time to express
her needs to them, and they became the representatives of
the priesthood in her home. Instead of feeling alienated,
judged, different, incomplete, and isolated, she felt completely accepted by her ward members.

Another divorced sister, however, was having many
problems in her home and felt resentful toward the Church.
She had a garden spot she wanted to use. Not having planted
before, she asked for help from her home teachers. Her request was not unreasonable. When the appointed time arrived, the home teacher was unable to come, so his wife
willingly went instead. The divorced sister answered the
door, handed the home teacher's wife the seeds, and pointed
to the garden; then she turned and closed the door!

Such an attitude invites alienation rather than oneness. It
says, "You are supposed to take care of me; it is your duty."
The other extreme is to be in great need but fearfully refuse
to seek help. Such an attitude deprives the person needing
help, and it also deprives others of the opportunity to serve.

Expressing genuine needs and sincerely seeking help is
often a way to humble oneself to accept counsel. Your responsibility is to give counsel that looks after immediate
needs as well as eternal goals and to teach self-reliance.

Several sisters, when asked how they were helped most
by their ward members, said:

"My bishop shakes my hand every Sunday, looks into my
eyes, and asks me how things are going."

"My visiting teacher calls me periodically just to check up
on me."

"My home teacher *always* follows through with the
things he says he'll do. If I don't hear back from him immediately, someone else follows up and gets back to me."

"I especially like the concern priesthood leaders express
and show to my children—especially my boys."

"Other families in the ward occasionally include me for
picnics or other activities. It's nice to feel included."

"My neighbors are so thoughtful. They make me feel secure in knowing that they are watching out for me."

"Holidays are particularly difficult for me. I've especially appreciated acts of love and concern at those times."

These comments are only a few of the ways people can help those who are divorced.

Counseling Techniques

The divorced person would not want to talk with you if he did not trust you. You need to continue to be worthy of that trust. Though we all make mistakes, the sincerity of your desire to help will carry you through many times when you may feel at a loss for the appropriate skills.

Frequently the divorced may seek your counsel on a topic that may seem minor. This may simply be an excuse to talk to you. Deeper concerns may lie just beneath the surface. If you suspect this to be the case, you may want to ask some questions that create an opportunity for the person to talk about his real feelings.

When working with specific problems, consider the need to involve the person's total family. Frequently, more cooperation is possible if everyone is aware of the details of a problem, especially if it is something that involves everyone, such as finances, household responsibilities, spirituality in the home, and so on. Assignments and commitments can be made and the differences resolved if everyone works together.

Where there is one problem, there may be many. It may be helpful to have the divorced person write down all of his concerns and then decide which ones he can do something about. (Sometimes people worry about things that cannot be changed or over which they have no control.)

For those things he can do something about, the person could:

1. Prioritize the problems.
2. Have them define the problems in clear terms.
3. Brainstorm alternative solutions to the problems (even those ideas that seem ridiculous may spawn new ideas).

4. Select the best solution and break it down into workable parts—specific things to do.

5. Commit to a time frame for accomplishing the tasks.

NOTE

1. Elisabeth Kübler-Ross, *On Death and Dying* (New York: MacMillan, 1969).

ABOUT THE AUTHOR

Jane C. Beuhring is presently a homemaker. Her educational background includes a bachelor's degree in home economics from Brigham Young University and studies toward a master's degree in marriage and family therapy from the same institution.

Mrs. Beuhring presently serves in her ward Relief Society presidency. In the past she has held various teaching positions. She has been a Young Special Interest leader on the ward, stake, and regional levels.

She and her husband, Ryan, are the parents of six children.

14

Parenting Alone

Suzanne Dastrup

Families with only one parent can be found in every unit of the Church. These families may be the result of divorce, death, or pregnancy out of wedlock. But all families with only one parent share a common difficulty—they must accomplish with one parent all that is generally accomplished by two.

The needs of the one-parent family vary from situation to situation. The family with young children may be seeking child-care services or occupational direction. The family with teenagers may need a loving ward member to help with Boy Scout merit badges or to fill an absent father's shoes on a daddy-daughter night. These specific needs will be different for each family. It is possible, however, to identify some general needs that apply to almost all single parent families.

First, one parent can't be both at home and at work. When the single parent is at work, her supervision and organization at home are not possible. If the single parent stays home, she has no source of income. Another problem is that when the single parent is thinking about work, she is not emotionally at home even if she is physically at home! Consequently, her home life suffers. And if she has to worry about her family while she is at work, her work may suffer.

Plumbing, gardening, yard care, budgeting, and automobile upkeep all need to be taken care of by someone, but then who is left to attend the children's school play, soccer game, or roadshow? Even in a two-parent family, covering all of the bases is a tough job. However, accomplishing all of these tasks with only one parent is even tougher.

Unburdening the Single Parent

The greatest need for the single parent is to be unburdened enough to be "emotionally available" to her children. The parent who is emotionally available in the home is one who listens, who responds with warmth and caring, who intervenes with direction and discipline, and who frequently radiates the Spirit in parent-child interactions. A parent is most able to be emotionally available to children when she is relatively free of worry and is inwardly confident and peaceful.

There are four specific difficulties in the single-parent home that may interfere with this parent-child relationship. These difficulties are responsibility overload, financial stress, bitterness, and isolation and self-doubt.

Responsibility Overload

The single parent is housekeeper, cook, breadwinner, seamstress, laundress, football coach, family referee, home evening lesson-preparer, family prayer organizer, plumber, mechanic, electrician, and gardener. But single parents do not necessarily have to be immobilized or constantly on edge because of responsibility overload. A more realistic vision of the main things they want to accomplish can alleviate some of the tension. Single parents should be congratulated on the multitude of tasks they complete each day. They should be encouraged to emphasize their accomplishments and not their failures.

It is generally true that one-parent families become discouraged by observing the two-parent families around them. This will lead to distress, guilt, and failure. One of the most important goals for single parents to achieve is to free themselves from comparisons with two-parent families.

Another goal is to find ways to take care of responsibilities that are not being fulfilled. Single parents should do everything they possibly can to manage the household, themselves, and their children. Having done this, they should then rely on extended family and ward or stake members to help with additional family responsibilities. These loved ones are called a *support system.*

Another support system is professionally trained social workers, counselors, and family therapists, whose skills and training can be helpful during any particularly stressful time.

A carefully selected live-in housekeeper can sometimes help a burdened single parent. This type of supportive involvement can free the parent to concentrate on his or her profession and children. Some single parents use members of their extended family (an aunt, sister, or mother) in a similar arrangement.

Relatives, home teachers, visiting teachers, friends, and neighbors may need to be told what specific things they can do to help. Often, people are afraid to serve others because they don't want to be "meddlers." The comment "Let me know what I can do . . ." is casually offered, but the desperately needed service is seldom rendered. Family and Church members may enjoy the blessing of service by looking for specific ways to help.

Financial Stress

A less easily solved problem for single parents is financial stress. Almost without exception, one of the first consequences of divorce is a reduction in family income. The income that originally supported just one household must now support two. (Financial stress is usually also a problem for the widow or widower.) Frequently the partner who is least qualified to earn a good income (the mother) is left with the major responsibility (the children). In such cases, poverty becomes a real problem. Poverty cannot be eliminated as easily as its effects can be understood and compensated for. Some of the negative effects of financial stress include the following.

1. Fewer luxuries or "extras" for the family (including recreation).

2. A change in residence, usually to smaller accommodations in an unfamiliar neighborhood.

3. Frequent moving, which contributes to parent and child insecurity.

4. Inability of the working parent to supervise her children.

Obviously, several of these negative effects can increase a child's insecurity. A move (or *several* moves) to a strange neighborhood adds many unknowns to a child's already upset world. Similarly, an abrupt reduction in quality of life-style can confuse and embitter a child. Inadequate supervision denies the child the structure and the boundaries he so desperately needs. When adequate child-care facilities are too expensive, a single parent often resorts to less effective means of supervision. Single parents most frequently rely on neighborhood teenagers as their full-time sitters. This is understandable for part-time care, but such full-time care may not provide the supervision and direction the child needs. Family and Church members could be informed of the need for help. Without proper supervision, the child is apt to suffer long-term confusion, rebellion, or lack of direction. Support systems can help minimize all the negative effects of financial stress.

Bitterness

For divorced, single parents, bitterness seems inevitable. During the first year following the divorce, most interactions between the divorced mother and father involve conflict over financial support, visitation arrangements, or child rearing. With time, however, these conflicts should decrease and the discussion of such issues should no longer be taken personally. The parents can be counseled to give up their defensiveness and to begin to increase their mutual cooperation. This cooperation is especially important for the children.

Divorced parents often express anger to their children. In their anguish, parents sometimes accuse their ex-spouse of any number of grievous sins. Such accusations may be accurate, but they may also be upsetting to a child. Some parents even make dishonest accusations. Children probably experience the most severe effects of bitterness when they are forced into such gossip sessions. Children naturally and wholesomely love both of their biological parents and should not be placed in a situation where they must deny their love for and loyalty to either of them. After a substantial adjustment period following a divorce, single parents should be counseled that cooperation with the former spouse will help the adjustment of everyone concerned. Cooperation may appear impossible at first, but an eternal perspective will allow a more compassionate view of an ex-spouse.

Love for the children is also shown through a cooperative relationship with the ex-spouse. When the parents are mature and friendly and arrange visits with the children with kindness and concern, there will be fewer emotional repercussions. This is not to say that divorces are based on love, but mud-slinging and backbiting could be eliminated with more satisfactory results for all concerned.

A second source of bitterness is loneliness and despair. By nature, people want to nurture, share, give, and receive in an eternal and complete family unit. These desires are righteous; they constitute the basic core of eternal identity. The periodic emergence of these unfulfilled desires results in a single parent's yearning and often in pain, resentment, and bitterness. The family's wish for completeness, the child's wish for a father or a mother, and the parent's wish for an eternal companion will probably reemerge for years to come. Single parents who do not remarry within two years following a divorce or the death of a spouse frequently report intense feelings of loneliness. This loneliness should not be incapacitating, but it should likewise not be denied, for it shows a refusal to give up an eternal family identity. Still, such loneliness may be difficult to endure, and the single parents may resign themselves to bitterness at the expense of patience, humility, and faith. Then they may not feel able to build good relationships with anyone.

Isolation and Self-Doubt

Isolation and subsequent self-doubt are another area of stress for single parents. Responsibility overload and financial stress each contribute to a single parent's isolation—lack of time and funds make it difficult for the person to have an adequate social life. Soon, the person begins to doubt her ability to build relationships with others, which leads to further isolation.

Isolation and self-doubt may also be the result of being single in a family-oriented world. The social stigma or stereotype of "the divorcee" or "the widower" may affect the single parent. Prejudices about single parents are sometimes held by misinformed or unaware people who feel it necessary to categorize people rather than accept them on their individual merit. However, this type of nonacceptance, in a Church unit or in a neighborhood, is usually more imagined than real. Because of this, it is valuable for single parents to be heavily involved in Church activities. This helps them to feel accepted by others.

Feeling inferior or out of place is certainly not the Lord's will for his children. We have been counseled "to give priority attention to single adults and their needs, to the extent that they will be properly involved in the mainstream of Church activity and will enjoy a foundation of growth and happiness in their Church association and personal lives." This quotation from "Guidelines for Single Adult Activities" distributed by the First Presidency in December 1979 emphasizes a need to reach out to members who are alone or lonely. Support from others can help lift single parents' burdens, free them to be emotionally available to their children, and strengthen them to be powerfully contributing Church members.

SUGGESTED READINGS

P. N. Clayton, "Meeting the Needs of the Single-Parent Family," *Family Coordinator* 20 (1971):327-36.

N. D. Colletta, "The Impact of Divorce: Father-Absence or Poverty?" *Journal of Divorce* 3 (1979):27-35.

D. S. Jacobson, "The Impact of Marital Separation/Divorce on Children," *Journal of Divorce* 1 (1978):341-59.

H. A. Mendes, "Single-Parent Families: A typology of Life Styles," *Social Work* 24 (1979):193-200.

B. Morris, "Counseling the Divorced L.D.S. Woman," *Journal of the Association of Mormon Counselors and Psychotherapists* 6 (1980):26-29.

R. Weiss, *Going It Alone* (New York: Basic Books, Inc., 1979).

J. D. West and F. Simone, "Counseling the Discouraged Single Parent," *Individual Psychologist* 16 (1979):48-53.

ABOUT THE AUTHOR

Suzanne Little Dastrup, a homemaker and single parent, received her bachelor's and master's degrees from Brigham Young University. She is presently nearing completion of her Ph.D. in marriage and family therapy from the same institution. An author and lecturer on single parents and reconstituted families, she has also been a counselor at the BYU Counseling Center and a family therapist at the Comprehensive Clinic at BYU.

Mrs. Dastrup is an active member of the Church. She has held positions in the Relief Society and has been YWMIA president, regional Young Special Interest leader, and Sunday School teacher.

She is the mother of three children.

15

Counseling Women
Ida Smith

Counseling women implies certain responsibilities that are not necessarily unique to counseling in Church settings but that are crucial to blessing the lives of women in the Church. Too often, women come away from counseling sessions feeling that they have not really been listened to, that they have not had an opportunity to state their entire problem before advice and counsel were given, that their concerns were not believed or were trivialized by the counselor. Considering this, here are some general guidelines for counseling with a woman: be honest with her; be a safe refuge for her; keep her confidences. At first, the support and understanding she receives from you will be more helpful than any information you could impart.

Typically, a woman will be grateful for your comfort and express appreciation for you. If you are a man, take care not to misread her gratitude and expression of care for you as being more than she intends. If her thankfulness were more than honest praise, she would be out of bounds in her feelings, and if you were to respond improperly, you would be dishonoring your responsibility. If your offer of help has been genuine, then you are representing the Savior in charity. If her response is honest, then she is communicating gratitude. It is not uncommon for a counselor or client to claim to have "fallen in love" with a person they are seeing. That kind of "love" is a counterfeit of genuine help. By being concerned but not inappropriately intimate, you can be an oasis of help and support.

Some Latter-day Saint women feel that certain situations generated by our culture put even greater pressure on them than on women generally. Many women simply need a place to express their feelings, assess their problems, and relieve themselves of burdens, with their counselors giving no comment, no judgment, no condemnation. Until a woman is allowed to do this, she will have little room in her mind for the principles and thoughts you may want to share. The counselor who has empathy, understanding, and compassion provides refuge for anyone in need of counseling.

As you acknowledge a woman's suffering, acknowledge also that it will diminish. The pain she feels does not need to continue at an intense level. It is important to first help reduce her pain; after her wounds are attended to, she will be less likely to lash out, inflicting suffering on herself as well as those around her. Do not talk down to her or say, "You shouldn't feel that way!" Such comments reveal more about your attitudes than about solutions to her problems. The feelings of those in emotional pain are real. If you believe, even subconsciously, that she is an inadequate person, your words and attitude will reveal it. Without your faith in her abilities and talents, without acknowledging her as capable, you have little to offer.

Sometimes a woman whose suffering is hidden may come for help. Her outward appearance, her standing in the Church or community, or her husband's position may hide her personal struggles. Many people put on a good facade. Take a woman's cries for help seriously; then you can assess how desperate she really may be.

Few problems develop overnight. A woman can be helped by understanding that she can grow out of a problem just as she grew into it. Like losing weight, psychological and emotional growth need to be measured in small increments. Sometimes just hanging on is progress, and the *desire to survive* is growth. When a woman has suffered serious depression and feels worthless, help her focus on just fifteen minutes of positive thinking each day, one day at a time, or to hold one happy thought or feeling every day. Acknowledging even one happy thought a *week* may be progress for some.

Help the woman to understand that it is not possible for you to make everything right for her. She must learn to do that for herself—with help and support from concerned others. Remember that often women have been raised in a way that promotes dependence on someone other than themselves. Often, that someone has been a man—father, husband, bishop, or stake president. By fostering her own capacities and self-reliance, you can help her take hold of her own life, including her own emotional health. You can explain this to her. Elder Boyd K. Packer has spoken of the need for Latter-day Saints to get off the spiritual dole.[1] This is especially true for women who have been socialized to be dependent on almost every level—physically, mentally, spiritually, and emotionally.

Be slow to advise and quick to support. Quick advice is often more judgmental than helpful. Support her in such a way that she will carry her own burdens. Be wary of the "shoulds" that you may not be authorized to suggest, such as "You should get married," "You should not work," or "You should move." Such prescriptions may ignore more fundamental principles the woman needs to learn, such as self-understanding and self-reliance.

Sometimes a woman who asks for counsel will be angry and depressed and not know why. You may find that her history of dependence has helped cause her to be angry with her husband; resentful of her children; rebellious toward priesthood, God, the Church, or any other authority. The solution to these feelings is one she may reject at first: she may need a closer relationship with God, a better understanding of her own identity, and a clearer sense of her spiritual mission. She needs to understand that the root of personal confidence is her own virtue, and that being a partner in her marriage is an important key to her own salvation. (D&C 132:20.)

The purpose of eternal marriage is that husband and

wife can grow into Godhood *together*. Marriage must be a partnership of equals. Contrary to culture or practice, woman is not meant to be a junior partner in marriage. President Spencer W. Kimball stated in his September 1978 address to women:

> Marriage is a partnership. Each is given a part of the work of life to do. The fact that some women and men disregard their work and their opportunities does not change the program. When we speak of marriage as a partnership, let us speak of marriage as a *full* partnership. We do not want our LDS women to be *silent* partners or *limited* partners in that eternal assignment! Please be a *contributing* and *full* partner.[2]

If a woman has not already assumed an equal partnership in her marriage, she should be encouraged and counseled to do so. This may include counseling with her husband, particularly if he sees the patriarchal role as one of domination and demands rather than one of loving persuasion and righteous influence as taught in Doctrine and Covenants 121.

Although you must recognize your own dependence on the Lord as you counsel, do not give the impression that all you say is of divine inspiration, unless it is and you have the authority to receive inspiration for that person. As one stake president said, "If you are inspired, say so! She needs to know it is the Lord speaking and not you alone. If you feel to advise, let the Lord do it through a blessing, but be *very* sure you are doing the right thing for her." Anyone who counsels has a profound responsibility to be righteous and to discern the will of the Lord.

When Men Counsel Women

The way a male counselor views his relationship with a female he is counseling is of vital importance. If he feels, however subtly, that he is superior to her or is just an extension of some other male in her life, he may give inappropriate advice. But if he sees his role as that of a teacher, guide, and one who has a right to bless her because of his Church position, then he is serving her best interests.

Some women may not have had good relationships with their fathers, husbands, or other men. We sometimes teach children that the love and concern our Heavenly Father has for us is like the love and concern of our earthly fathers. But if a woman has not enjoyed the love of an earthly father or husband, she will not have had that example to teach her about a loving Heavenly Father. Your words and actions should help her better envision Him. The scriptures counsel that if we cannot learn to love our imperfect brothers, neighbors, husbands, and others whom we have seen, we cannot claim to love God whom we have not seen. (See 1 John 4:20-21.)

What if a woman is married to a tyrannical husband who misuses his priesthood? What is her responsibility? Ideally, of course, it would be to forgive him. This does not mean she should become a doormat to his unrighteousness. It simply means that she will do all in her power to pursue a right course of action herself. Her coming to you with a marital problem grounded in the unrighteous dominion of her husband is in itself righteous and responsible. If she has come alone, it is naive to think that her marital problems will be solved by the two of you alone. A husband must repent of his unrighteousness if his marriage is to be healed. If the husband does not abandon his tyranny, there will be no solution.

Too many wives suffer the unrighteous dominion of men who dishonor their priesthood. Sometimes a man uses "priesthood" to belittle, control, or even physically abuse a woman. If the woman has difficulty in separating *man* from *priesthood*, help her see that unrighteous behavior of such a man means "amen" to his priesthood or authority. (See D&C 121:34-37.) When there is such unrighteousness, it does not mean that there is no hope for the future. On the contrary, when husbands and wives repent and forgive, they can solve their problems. Your task is to work toward that goal. This usually means that, at some point, the husband of a woman will also need to be involved in counseling with you.

Priesthood gives men the governing power in the Church. Men may need to be counseled that this does not make them better, smarter, more blessed, more capable of making correct decisions, more inspired, more logical, or more loved of God than are women.

Righteous priesthood holders recognize the true status of women and know they are equal to men in spiritual power, divine potential, and responsibility for their callings. Women need to know that they have just as much right to inspiration as men do. But often they do not understand their right to inspiration and revelation and therefore receive none, because they expect none. Help the women you counsel to recognize their own right to receive personal revelation. You might ask, "What is *your* recommendation in this situation?" You might suggest, "The Lord will reveal your responsibility to you, so let's examine *your* reservoir of help." Women have great recuperative powers, and they must learn to draw upon the Lord for their strength.

Help each woman you counsel to understand agency and how to choose the right. Encourage her to study the scriptures and to do her own thinking. If she is depressed, sees herself in an inferior position, or is angry, she may feel incapable of praying to a God who she thinks neither hears her nor cares about her. But such negative feelings can be left behind as she feels the Lord's love and guidance.

President Spencer W. Kimball has urged the sisters of the Church to become gospel scholars. They deserve to be challenged to learn and teach correct doctrine. Occasionally leaders ask only the husband to speak on doctrinal subjects in sacrament meeting while they ask the wife to speak about her family. Such assignments will tend to weaken, not strengthen, the woman's resolve to become a gospel scholar.

The family dimension of a woman's gospel scholarship is especially crucial. Pearl Buck's statement that "no man ever recovers fully from the ignorance of his mother" may be even more serious if the ignorance is spiritual. To underestimate the importance of the woman's spiritual influence in the home is disastrous. Though a husband and father should be a spiritual leader in the home, the wife and mother has an equal responsibility to develop her spiritual leadership.

Myths about Women

There are a number of myths that may distract the counselor, the woman he counsels, or both. One such myth is that priesthood leaders have ready answers to questions about family size. Such concerns should be the responsibility of a wife and a husband with the Lord. Basic questions such as whether to use birth control and how often to have children should be taken to the Lord by a woman and her husband. Different couples may receive different answers concerning their questions.[3] How many children other families have is irrelevant. The counsel from the First Presidency on these matters emphasizes the personal nature of these decisions.

Another myth is that if anything goes wrong with the spiritual or emotional climate of the home, the woman is to blame. Blame never solves problems. Whether a woman blames herself or her husband blames her, neither is solving the problem of what the climate in the home should be. In fact, the very blaming causes a bad climate.

A woman may hesitate to say anything she feels might diminish or belittle her husband in your eyes. If a counselor is not equipped to help her speak freely, he may want to direct her to someone who can. He may also need to help her learn to talk to her husband in new or different ways. He might say, "Are you willing to try a different line of communication?" or "What might you say instead?" or "I know you don't want to be in an inferior position. Let's practice saying what you feel in another way."

A woman may benefit from learning to talk honestly and straightforwardly with her husband about her feelings. For example, a woman who has been quietly accepting undue criticism from her husband for a long time may want to change this negative pattern. She needs to tell her husband in a frank but loving way that she does not like being put down, that being criticized hurts her, and that it is harming their relationship. She might say to him that she realizes only he can change his behavior, but that she wants him to know what his negative behavior means to her.[4]

It is a myth that every Latter-day Saint woman should

somehow fit into the same mold. Help the women you counsel to understand that they do not have to compete with other Latter-day Saint women! Stress their individuality and urge them not to compare their family, husband, or children with anyone else's. Being good at some things and mediocre at others is typical of most people. God asks us to strive for perfection, but he does not require perfection before he extends his love to us. But as we become perfect *in love*, then other kinds of progress or perfection follow. When women compare themselves to others, they lose sight of the very principles they are striving to live, and they miss opportunities to either learn from the strengths of others or to help those with other needs.

Every woman is different from every other woman, and has different needs at the various stages of her life. For example, if the woman you counseled to get married at age twenty-one is still single at age thirty-five, you may find it more appropriate to support her in her career choice than to harp on the theme "You ought to get married!" Carrying out such counsel is hardly something she can do alone. Counseling a woman to stay home and not work may be appropriate for a young mother with small children but inappropriate for a woman of forty-five whose children are grown. Such counsel should focus on general principles regarding family and work commitments; it should rarely involve specific prescriptions. A woman's interests and talents that are a blessing to her family can be offered outside the home as well. To take such talents beyond the walls of her home does not mean she is disobedient, a bad mother, or a marginal Church member. Nor is it wrong for a woman to limit her influence to the home. In summary, there is joy to be found in the diversity of opportunity available to women. They can approach such opportunities faithfully, prayerfully, and individually.

It is a myth that a woman who raises questions is automatically on the road to apostasy. Women in the Church today are asking many questions about doctrine and Church procedures, just as men are. Think of women who raise questions as people who are willing to discuss their thoughts, not as someone in rebellion. Ask yourself, "Would I be upset, concerned, or feel threatened if this question were coming from a man, or would I merely discuss it with him and then try to find an answer?" If a woman is to be responsible for her own salvation and is to get off the spiritual dole, she needs to ask honest questions and seek honest answers. Honesty in questioning, not the questioning itself, is the key to progress.

It is a myth that building only faith is sufficient to help someone. If a woman is told that fasting and prayer alone will solve her problems, and then she does fast and pray and the problems are not solved because she still lacks the skills to solve her problems, her guilt is likely to increase; her depression will then become more acute, and it will be that much more difficult to help her out of the negative cycle she is experiencing. She may need tools or skills to help her solve her problems. For example, suppose a couple were called on a mission and were assigned to an area where driving a car was essential in their work and the woman did not know how to drive a car. She would not be told to go home and pray about it. This would be only the beginning of a solution to her problem. Someone would need to *teach* her how to drive a car, and then she should pray that she might use the new skill safely and correctly. Similarly, if a woman lacks skills in dealing with those around her, she deserves help in learning those skills. Fasting and prayer can be far more effective when the person needing help has been given tools and skills that the Lord can then help her use to solve her problems.

Single Women and Decisions about Marriage

Approximately one in six women do not marry, and many more become divorced or widowed. One-third of the adult women in the United States do not have a man in the home to support them. Though Latter-day Saint women *do* understand the importance of families and family systems, not all of them will marry, bear children, and have their own families in mortality. Most single Latter-day Saint women would prefer to be married if they could, and therefore do not constantly need to be told that they should be. A woman is not obliged to accept a proposal of marriage to a man she does not love or wish to be with throughout eternity. Joseph Fielding Smith wrote in "Elijah the Prophet and His Mission," published in the *Utah Genealogical and Historical Magazine*, January 1921:

> You good sisters, who are single and alone, do not fear, do not feel that blessings are going to be withheld from you. You are not under any obligation or necessity of accepting some proposal that comes to you which is distasteful for fear you will come under condemnation. If in your hearts you feel that the Gospel is true, and would under proper conditions receive these ordinances and sealing blessings in the temple of the Lord, and that is your faith and your hope and your desire, and if that does not come to you now, the Lord will make it up, and you shall be blessed—for no blessing shall be withheld.

In his talk to women in September 1979, President Kimball said:

> Sometimes to be tested and proved requires that we be temporarily deprived—but righteous women and men will one day receive *all*—think of it, sisters—*all* that our Father has! It is not only worth waiting for; it is worth living for!
>
> Meanwhile, one does not need to be married or a mother in order to keep the first and second great commandments—those of loving God and our fellowmen—on which Jesus said hang all the law and all the prophets.[5]

Being single need not inhibit a single woman's efforts to strive for exaltation. A woman who is single, who has no immediate marriage plans, and who seeks a career or advanced degree is not necessarily making a negative statement about marriage. She is probably taking intelligent steps to ensure her own survival, success, and happiness.

Older single women should be supported in their singleness. They need to know that it is all right to be alone; being single may be second choice, but it is not the end of the world. Yes, families are first. But not all women *can* be married, since in the twenty-and-over population women outnumber men in the United States by 8.6 million.

It is not only permissible for women to be single and happy at the same time, but crucial that women of every age find resources that will ensure their happiness whatever their marital status. Helping older single women to adjust in a positive and creative way to this reality calls for insight, understanding, prayer, and freedom from prejudice in the counselor.

If a counselor has the attitude that a woman is not available to do the Lord's work until some condition in her life changes—until she gets married, remarries, and so on—then the counseling may have an unintended debilitating effect. It is important to remember that every woman, no matter what her marital status, has an earthly mission to perform. This may or may not be in ways that we traditionally think of women serving the Lord. The outcome of any counseling should be to help her, through continual righteous living, to discern directions available to her that are consistent with the Lord's will.

Counseling Women Who Work

Many Latter-day Saint women work outside the home. Many are mothers with small children still at home. The vast majority of such women are working for compelling economic reasons and are in great need of support and encouragement. Specific counsel on when to work is usually overstepping your responsibilities, but many men and women are concerned about the consequences of wives' working. When they seek your help about such matters, teach correct principles. Have husbands and wives examine their own hearts on such sensitive decisions. Whatever their decisions, your role is not to condemn. Children deserve to know of the family financial circumstances and why their mother is working. A mother's going to work can be an act of love for her children, and they should be helped to understand this. Children can then be a source of support as the family works through its financial difficulties together. The issue is always what would be best for the family. Again, women and their situations differ widely, and what may be appropriate for one might not be for another. Women with an "empty nest" might greatly enhance their lives by working outside the home.

Education for Women

At a Paris area conference in 1977, Sister Camilla Kimball said:

> I would hope that every girl and woman here has the desire and ambition to qualify in two vocations—that of homemaking, and that of preparing to earn a living outside the home, if and when the occasion requires. An unmarried woman is always happier if she has a vocation in which she can be socially of service and financially independent. . . . Any married woman may become a widow without warning. Property may vanish as readily as a husband may die. Thus, any woman may be under the necessity of earning her living and helping to support dependent children. If she has been trained for the duties and emergencies of life which may come to her, she will be much happier and have a greater sense of security.[6]

Fortunate is the young woman who received counsel and encouragement in her youth as to the importance of preparing to take care of herself—and then did. Many women have not so prepared, however, and when they find themselves suddenly widowed or divorced, they do not have the necessary skills to support themselves, let alone their children. Teenage girls who become mothers before age seventeen rarely finish high school and frequently find themselves having to rely on Church or state welfare. Many older women who are left with no husband to support them are locked into low-paying or dead-end jobs because they have acquired no marketable skills. As difficult as it may be for these women to take the time to acquire such skills, three or four years of schooling in their twenties, thirties, or forties can be a great hedge against a life of poverty or welfare dependence. The government now estimates it will cost over $135,000 to raise one child to age eighteen. The financial implications to individual, Church, and state are obvious.

With a woman's life span now seventy-nine years, most mothers will find themselves with twenty to forty years left after their children are grown and gone. Those who find themselves with time weighing heavily on their hands after years of rearing children might be encouraged to go back to school to broaden their experiences through further education.

Traumatic Changes

Major changes in women's lives, such as childbirth, death of a loved one, divorce, or a move, may take up to three years to adjust to. Sometimes putting a woman in touch with another woman who has faced and survived similar experiences may be very helpful to her, depending on the maturity of those she might talk with. Some of these experiences are discussed below.

Divorce

Divorced women are particularly vulnerable to outside influences because they are often forced into the working world for reasons of financial survival. Many are unprepared for the fact that even some Latter-day Saint men might treat women unfairly. Some men feel that they should make all decisions and be in charge even though they may sometimes defer to a woman (often in a condescending way). Also, there may be times when they are patronizing or unnecessarily distant in relationships with women who are not related to them.

Some Latter-day Saint women find that some men who are not Church members listen to them, admire them, are likely to treat them as equals, are socially at ease with them, and are great fun. Such women, therefore, may think they are safe with these men when sometimes they are *not!* Some nonmember men are agreeable, sharing, and accepting, but many lean toward a relaxed moral standard, and divorced or widowed Latter-day Saint women are often vulnerable and ill equipped to deal with these men and their standards. In some geographic areas or other circumstances nonmembers may be the only marriageable men available, and so the social life of single Latter-day Saint women will suffer as a result. Latter-day Saint women in these circumstances should not give up their standards, and might need to be counseled not to become involved in situations "over their heads."

Abuse

If a woman complains of abuse—mental or physical—believe her. To assume that she "asked for it" or "deserved it" would be incredibly un-Christlike. There is no excuse—ever—for abuse, and it should not be tolerated in any form. It is not possible for a woman to have true love and trust for any person who abuses her. Certainly the abuser has as great a need to receive counseling as the person who is abused. Dismissing complaints as exaggerated or as too bizarre to be real may cause you to overlook a nest of real problems. As you develop your questioning skills, you may discover problems more serious than a woman is at first willing to disclose.

Whatever form the abuse has taken, her self-esteem is likely to be extremely low or even nonexistent. It will undoubtedly take time and a great amount of positive reinforcement from you and others to help her begin to see herself and her life in a positive light.

Excommunication or Disfellowshipment

As a sister unfolds her story, you may see that her problems arise from serious sins that will demand considerable repentance and demand court action such as disfellowshipment or excommunication. Even when such action is necessary, it is important that the woman feel loved and accepted and that she know that both you and the Lord can hate her sin but still love her. A woman facing Church court action needs assurance that she can be helped and that all is not lost. Women in despair must feel there can be room for them in the Church, no matter how serious their problems. Some women who are in deep depression, not knowing who they are or where they stand in God's eyes, may need loving support to learn that simply leaving the Church is *not* the right or only solution to their problems. No matter how serious a woman's situation is, help her to use it as a steppingstone back into the Church.

More Responses and Resources

As you counsel, you will recognize that some women are emotionally or psychologically impaired. If you sense a strong need to refer such a woman to a professional counselor, be sure she understands that you feel good about her getting it. There is no stigma attached to seeking professional counseling.

Lay counselors need to be realistic and modest about their own abilities and time commitments. It is all right to say, "I don't know," and to recognize that the person being counseled needs either more help or a different kind of help than you are prepared to give.

Among the professionals you have to call upon, be sure you have some who can be reached in emergencies after hours. Some counseling services are available only from eight-to-five Monday through Friday. As you become familiar with the counseling resources in your community, you can build relationships with professionals you trust and who are sympathetic to the needs of Latter-day Saints.

There are different kinds of counseling needs: medical, psychological, and spiritual. If, as you work with a woman, you find that she exhibits bizarre behavior, that together you cannot find any reason for her behavior, that her problems have a set pattern and have gone on for a long time, that she comes to you over and over and seems not to be making any progress, or that you cannot help her discern her responsibility for her own worth, value, and actions, you may wish to seek assistance at a professional level. It is important, however, that you still remain available to her for counsel.

Summary

Ultimately, of course, happiness lies within the individual. Others may help, but ultimately each woman is responsible for her own positive relationships with herself and with the world. The goal of every Latter-day Saint woman should be to find joy in this life, to become strong, and to learn to take responsibility for her own growth. The men in a woman's life need to wholeheartedly affirm her in such righteous efforts. Eternal relationships of men and women should be based on the strength of both, and any counseling with women should reflect that goal.

NOTES

1. *Ensign*, 8 (May 1978): 91-93.

2. Emphasis by President Spencer W. Kimball, *Ensign* 8 (November 1978): 106.

3. *Ensign,* 9 (August 1979): 23–24.

4. C. Kay Allen, *Journey from Fear to Love* (Denver, Colorado: Human Values Institute, 1980).

5. Spencer W. Kimball, "The Role of Righteous Women," *Ensign* 9 (November 1979):103.

6. Camilla Kimball, "A Woman's Preparation," *Ensign* 7 (March 1977): 59.

SUGGESTED READINGS

C. Kay Allen, *Journey from Fear to Love* (Denver, Colorado: Human Values Institute, 1980).

Carlfred Broderick, *Couples* (New York: Simon & Schuster, 1979).

Sterling Ellsworth, *Tale of Two Selves* (Ellsworth Printing, 1978).

ABOUT THE AUTHOR

Ida Smith, former director of the Women's Research Institute at Brigham Young University, holds a bachelor's degree in political science from the University of Utah. Having had many years of experience in education, business, and industry before coming to BYU, she has coordinated research projects concerning women's issues and consulted with women's organizations on the needs of women in the Church. She now serves with the BYU alumni office.

Sister Smith has spoken to over a hundred different groups between 1979 and 1983 on topics relating to women's concerns.

She has held numerous ward, stake, and regional callings, including gospel doctrine teacher, mother education teacher, counselor in a Young Women's presidency, and Special Interest stake and regional chairman.

16

Aging

J. Richard Connelly

Most of us deny the aging process. As we get older, we sometimes refuse to admit that we don't see or hear as well as when we were young, and even if we admit it, we avoid getting glasses or asking people to speak up unless it is absolutely necessary. But old age comes, perhaps earlier than we expect it. The most rapid decline in the five senses—vision, hearing, taste, touch, and smell—occurs between forty and sixty years of age; however, these deficits are usually associated with people much older. Fortunately, because of the adaptability and the extra abilities possessed by most people, inability to cope and severe disabilities do not occur until seventy-five years of age or later. Yet community and even church programs often separate, stereotype, and stigmatize older people.

We need to analyze our attitudes about aging and the aged. When you see a person fifty years of age, do you see a person whose life is half over or one who has half his life yet to live? When you look at yourself in the mirror, do you see signs and marks of a life lived and appreciated or do you regret the passage of time? Would you like to return to your younger years?

Who is old? Is it a ninety-year-old woman who says that she will not participate in a senior citizens center or the Church's Special Interest program because that's where all the old folks are? Is it the sixty-five-year-old who complains about retirement, about his children, about the way society deals with older people? Or is it the woman who is twenty, thirty, or forty years old who complains about what the passage of time has done to her? Many people believe that the only people who are old are those who are older than themselves. Other people consider themselves old if others define and treat them as being old.

When I was working with elderly Indians in Arizona, a seventy-one-year-old Navajo woman said to me, "I didn't know that I was old until last fall when I was picking an apple off my tree and fell down. As I lay on the ground, I realized that no one had pushed me. I did not trip over a stone. I simply fell down. And, as I looked to the heavens, I said, 'Lord, I must be getting old.'" That statement was confirmed when a few days later a worker with a nutrition program for the elderly called at her home. The worker said, "Irene, you qualify as a senior citizen, and we would like to have you come to our nutrition site and enjoy a good meal and socialize with others who are there." Irene had fallen, someone had said she was a senior citizen, so she decided maybe she was old.

Being old is a perception and an attitude. Some people who are chronologically in their nineties display youthful attitudes, intellect, and enthusiasm, and stay in good physical condition. It is up to each person to decide if he will let others influence the way he perceives his later years.

On the other hand, being old is also a time in life when people lose loved ones, lose physical agility, and must depend more on others. They often cause families, neighbors, Church members, and the community to face diseases— often deteriorative—and circumstances they have never dealt with before.

Nevertheless, it is important to understand that there are greater differences among older people than there are similarities. No two people are the same. The freedom we allow and the encouragement we give to people of all ages is critical to building the self-awareness, self-esteem, and independence of older people. We sometimes tend to lump people together, to force all people of certain ages into similar molds. But people are more individualistic and unique when they are older than they were when they were younger. As you are around and work with older people, be sensitive to their uniqueness, for it is impressive, and it is also one of their strengths.

Challenges of Older People

There are two general groups of older people. The first group is the "Young-Old" (from fifty-five to seventy-four years of age) and the other is the "Vulnerable-Old" seventy-five years of age and older).

The challenges of the Young-Old group include at least the following:

1. Preparing for and adjusting to retirement.

2. Anticipating and adjusting to lower and fixed incomes after retirement.

3. Establishing satisfactory physical living arrangements.

4. Adjusting to new relationships with adult children and their offspring.

5. Learning or continuing to develop leisure time activities to help replace role losses.

6. Anticipating and adjusting to slower physical and intellectual responses.

7. Dealing with the death of parents, spouses, and friends.

The Young-Old people can be a powerful force in changing laws that will assure that they benefit from an economic system they contributed to for so long. They can also be a great force to be called upon in the Church to help others who are in difficulty; to advise, counsel, and teach the young. Their experiences have given them administrative knowledge, family wisdom, and solutions to many problems. However, time demands on the Young-Old must be offered with the same reverence, prayer, and respect due those of any age group. In addition, a sensitivity to their age limitations, family commitments, and so on is crucial. To assume

that a retired couple would be ideal to serve in a nursery or
that they should usually tend their grandchildren may be incorrect.

The other group of people, the Vulnerable-Old, often suffer from loss of hearing or sight. They may have various ar-
thritic or respiratory ailments. Many suffer from some form
of cardiac decompensation or from kidney and bladder
problems. Diabetes is another common problem of this
group. Yet these people continue to survive despite these
losses, and are often happy and cheerful.

People over seventy-five face the following tasks and
challenges:

1. Learning to combine their growing dependency on
others with their continuing need for independence.

2. Adapting to living alone.

3. Learning to accept and adjust to possible in-home services or institutional living (nursing homes).

4. Establishing an affiliation with their age group.

5. Learning to adjust to heightened vulnerability to physical and emotional stress.

6. Adjusting to losses of spouse, home, and friends.

7. Adjusting to the loss of physical strength, to increased
illness, and to the approach of death.

The Vulnerable-Old have more difficulty than the Young-
Old in making friends, maintaining old friendships, and
contributing what they would consider their fair share toward church, neighborhood, and community activities.
They frequently suffer from isolation—more social isolation
than geographic isolation. Their need to be needed is strong
and presents a challenge that a counselor can help creatively
fill.

To accurately assess the needs of older people is difficult.
But if we focus on their tasks and challenges, understand the
personality changes that occur with the passage of time, and
then learn about the physical changes of old age, we will
have a better chance to deal with problems of the aging more
effectively.

Personality Changes

Research indicates that with increasing old age, people's thoughts turn inward. People change from active to passive ways of controlling their environments. Developmental psychologists call this an increased "inferiority" of personality. There are some differences in aging between men and women. Men seem to become more receptive to group activities and more nurturant. They also appear to cope with the environment in increasingly abstract and intellectual ways. Women seem to become more assertive and less guilty about being so. They also increase in their feelings and their expression of those feelings. It is not clear whether personality changes are due to the passage of time (aging) and its accompanying physical and biological changes or if they are due to how society deals with older people. Major physical and mental health problems sometimes affect the personality in ways that influence the older person's family to want to avoid him or even deny his existence.

Senility

The label "senile," as used by most people in our society, describes a person who is old, confused, forgetful, emotionally unstable, stubborn, or disagreeable. If a person is *young* and strong-minded, he is labeled "headstrong" or "aggressive." But if he is *old* and strong-minded, he is sometimes labeled "stubborn." If he is young and forgets a place, or the time, he simply forgot or had too many things on his mind. But if he is old and forgets something, he is "senile." Some people even believe that senility is a natural process of aging ("Well, you can't expect anything different from someone his age") or that it is irreversible ("Well, there is nothing we can do for her now; she's old and senile"), and that if an older person is not senile, he is an exception.

All of these perceptions are inaccurate. In fact, *senility* is not a medical term. The medical term is *senile dementia* or *senile psychosis*, also known as *organic brain syndromes*. Organic brain syndromes generally affect five areas: (1) judgment (impaired); (2) feelings (instability or shallowness); (3) memory (usually short-term); (4) confusion (spotty, worse at night); (5) orientation (to time, place, or person). These five symptoms occur when there is a lack of blood flowing to the brain cells. The blood carries oxygen and nutrients that activate and maintain the brain cells.

True senile dementia occurs when brain cells die. This condition occurs largely because of cerebral arteriosclerosis, or hardening and narrowing of the arteries. With this hardening, less blood is able to flow into all parts of the brain, and without adequate nourishment, some brain cells die. Senile dementia may also be caused by primary degenerative disease of the brain.

There is a major problem in making an accurate diagnosis of senility, because other causes may restrict the flow of blood or the amount of oxygen or nutrients in the blood that feed the brain cells, such causes as congestive heart failure, malnutrition, infection, stroke, combination or overdose of drugs, head trauma, alcoholism, anxiety, and depression. All of these causes, however, are treatable and therefore reversible. Only in cases of true senile dementia (approximately 2 percent of older people) is the condition irreversible.

To assure the family and yourself as a counselor that a diagnosis of senile dementia is accurate, you should select a physician trained in geriatric medicine and consult with a geriatric nurse clinician.

Depression
Older people who are frequently depressed appear to be suffering from chronic brain syndrome. They seem disoriented, confused, and show memory losses. Because there is a steady rise in depressive conditions with advancing age, depression is a common complaint among the elderly. Social, psychological, and physical changes of old age create difficult problems and make the aged person vulnerable to frustration, failure, grief, disappointment, and apathy. Physical losses and disturbances in the brain may maintain and increase the depressive state.

Loss of physical health is often depressive, so a counselor should look to prevention and early detection of illness. Depressive states in the elderly often go unnoticed, perhaps because many people assume that older people are by nature somewhat confused and apathetic. This expectation that older people are senile masks the depression.

Important points to consider about depression in older people include the following:

1. The aged may have difficulty dealing with physical health and social-psychological losses. There is a close link between physical health and mental health. Pay careful attention to the extent of vision and hearing loss, ability to move around, and loss of status. Helping the older person substitute or compensate for such losses will help reduce depression.

2. Anxiety, insomnia, lack of proper nutrition, and energy loss may indicate an underlying depression and, in addition, may contribute to its continuation.

3. Depressions may mimic organic brain syndrome.

4. Apathy is characteristic of depression in the later years.

5. Depressed people are usually not disoriented.

6. Medications can bring about depression.

Help the older person with depression from loss of status and self-worth to find an activity of genuine interest and to develop relationships with others. Work with the person's family, with his ward members, with his neighbors, and with the community. With more severe depression (because of death of a loved one, serious illness, or other losses), help the person find an "intimate confidant," a person who will be an active listener. The release of grief and anger is liberating, but it is not enough. Listening should be combined with encouragement and reinforcement to help the person establish self-awareness and self-worth.

Loneliness

Clark E. Moustakas said in his book *Loneliness* (Englewood Cliffs: Prentice-Hall, 1961), "Elder citizens in our society are particularly affected by the social and cultural changes and by the separation, urbanization, alienation, and automation in modern living. There is no longer a place for old age, no feeling of organic belonging, no reverence or respect, or regard for the wisdom and talent of the ancient." Our elder citizens often have feelings of uselessness and conclude that life is utterly futile. The fear of death is common among old people. Losses in the later years of life are realities. Loneliness among the elderly may be caused by the death of a spouse, a sibling, a close neighbor, a roommate, or anyone who has been important to him. Loneliness is often revisited on the birthdays, anniversaries, and the death date of those who have died. However, the memories of these people can be enriching. Pets are often important to older people, and the loss of a pet often makes life lonelier for an aging person.

People from different ethnic backgrounds, particularly those in America who can't speak English, often feel isolated and alone. The pains and aches of rheumatism and arthritis, though common, may produce a feeling of being alone. There are certain times of the day and certain times of the year that are more difficult to live through than others. Holidays often create loneliness for elderly people who are widowed. Making major decisions (and sometimes minor decisions) like buying a car or an appliance often creates a lonely feeling in someone who has for years made those decisions with a spouse or someone else who has died.

Loneliness can be difficult to treat mainly because it is an individual matter and deeply rooted in the self-esteem of a person. Constant effort should be made to bolster the person's self-esteem through frequent contact and acknowledgment on difficult days. Acknowledgment and praise for the smallest gain or positive change in an older person's behavior bolsters his self-image and lets him know that someone cares.

In relationships with older people, we should be willing to experiment in trying to help those who are lonely. We should be creative in our approaches and encourage inter-

action of those who are lonely with other people of all ages
and in all kinds of activities.

Chronic Illness

The number of people between the ages of fifty-five and
sixty-five who have one or more chronic conditions sky-
rockets. Among the population forty-five to sixty-four years
of age, about seventy-two percent have one or more chronic
conditions. That percentage increases to 86 percent among
the population sixty-five years of age and older. Among the
elderly, multiple chronic conditions are common. These
conditions generally include mental illness, diabetes, arthritis, rheumatic disease, heart and circulatory disorders,
and vision and hearing impairments.

Many diseases manifest themselves after age sixty-five
because they are consequences of changes in the body
brought on by slow, progressive, deteriorative conditions.
People do not get sick just because they are old; old people
get sick because many disease processes start early but become more likely to cause illness the longer they last.

Despite their many chronic health problems that develop
with increasing age, most older people do not consider
themselves to be seriously handicapped in pursuing their or-
dinary daily activities. Though four out of five persons who
are sixty-five years of age and over suffer from at least one
chronic medical condition, less than one in five report that
they are severely handicapped or that they are unable to
carry on major daily activities. Generally, most elderly
people rate their health as fair, good, or excellent rather than
as poor.

The best way to help people with chronic illnesses is to be
supportive and help them manage their disease. We can help
with shopping and provide encouragement, companionship, transportation, and help with illnesses or disabilities.
We can learn about community support agencies and get
help from medical and health professionals in emergencies.
Treatment of one disease without knowledge of the other
diseases that might accompany it could be disastrous. We

should encourage the use of a reputable physician trained in geriatrics and a chemical pharmacist who sees older people regularly and knows their disease and drug histories.

Deciding to Use a Long-Term Care Facility

When should an older person in need of care be placed in a long-term care facility, and when should that person continue to live in the community? Families and older individuals are plagued with this question constantly. It can never be answered in a simple way. The answer depends on the person and must be based on the community resources that are available.

Community Services

Services available to the older population range from preventive services to institutional living. Services are medical and nonmedical. Eighty different programs are funded by the federal government alone. Most of these programs are available in every state in the nation and in most communities. Some services may not be available, but Area Agencies on Aging (AAA) cover small geographical areas within each state. In addition, State Unit on Aging can be contacted for referral.

Preventive services include health screening clinics or health screening activities. These may be carried on at various places. Elderly people receive glaucoma, podiatry, blood pressure, and other types of screening. Early detection is important in the treatment and control of disease. Physical and mental health education is available, as well as general education. Almost every community has an information and referral service for the aged. Through this service, people are directed to the most appropriate service agency.

In-home services include home repairs, shopping assistance, meals on wheels, friendly visitors, volunteer services, telephone reassurance, homemakers, chore services, and home health services. These services are usually inexpensive and can help maintain an older person without placing him in an institution.

Community services range from social and recreational clubs to community mental health centers. Often the Area Agency on Aging or a community services council maintains a directory listing all the community agencies and the services they deliver. The directories are often free or may be purchased for a nominal fee.

Community living includes homes and other living arrangements that can provide support and social interaction for an older person. Hospice organizations provide support for a dying person and their families. This support can be delivered as in-home services or as services within a hospice. The professional services allow an older person to die at home or at least outside a hospital.

Institutional living includes intermediate care facilities, which generally have nursing staffs that are present only during the day, whereas the other types of institutions in this category have nursing and often other health disciplines represented twenty-four hours a day. Only 5 to 6 percent of the population sixty years of age and older are in nursing homes at any one time in the United States, but there is about a 22 percent chance that an older person will spend some time as a patient in a nursing home during his lifetime.

Deciding to Use Services for the Aged

There is no one moment when a decision to use services for the aged should be made. The decision should be a continual one beginning when a need for service first becomes evident. The elderly person and his family members should discuss the possibility of using these services. Few older people receive careful preparation. They should always be asked to participate in making the decision, as this is a critical factor in their subsequent adjustment and well-being. New decisions should reflect changes in individual and family circumstances. Options created by new legislation and the development of new services also encourage additional decisions.

Assessment of individual and family circumstances can be done by the family, by local church leaders, by neighbors, and by friends. Professionals in the field should also be relied upon to help assess functioning levels of the older person and to suggest appropriate placements and to monitor adjustments and future changes.

Conditions that promote institutionalization are usually advanced old age; multiple physical and mental impairments; and lack of economic, family, and social support. The financial resources available to a person from his own private sources, from family, and from federal programs often determine whether he can take advantage of some of the services he needs. In some cases, the most appropriate placement cannot be made because of financial limitations. The eligibility criteria, the range of benefits, and the administrative and admissions arrangements of community agencies and services often control the decision for services.

Family Involvement

The family is usually the first to observe changes in the mental and physical health of the elderly. In assessing those changes, the family usually seeks advice from others and is likely to assume responsibility for planning the future of the older person. The assumption may prevail that the family should make all the decisions and arrangements. But someone, whether it be a professional social worker, a nurse, a physician, a bishop, or a Church Social Services worker, needs to see that the planning is carried out *with* the older person. This helper needs to respond to the family's request for information and discussion of the situation, but the older person should be consulted as early as possible.

In most cases, families are interested and concerned about their elderly parent or relation. Families should not, and usually do not, "dump" their elderly into institutions. Research indicates that family ties continue to be viable, adult children continue to behave responsibly, and the placing of an elderly relative is the last rather than the first resort of families. In general, families exhaust all other alternatives and often endure severe personal, social, and economic stresses in the process, ending up making the final

decision with the utmost reluctance, often with feelings of
guilt. To put it another way, there is much evidence of
genuine affection and loyalty between institutionalized
older people and their children.

The family is interested in the welfare of their older relative but often are unknowledgeable and fearful. It is impera-
tive that others involved in planning help the family work
through their feelings. The family is often disheartened, unhappy, frightened, and guilty. Adult children feel that they
are rejecting their aged parents. These feelings come even
when the only possible solution is institutionalization.

Some family members find it too painful to watch the deterioration of an older loved one or maintain a distance because of unresolved conflicts. Families may find it difficult to
visit long-term care facilities or to watch the degenerative
process that changes the personality and appearance of their
loved ones.

If institutions cannot be avoided, it is important that the
entire family be encouraged to continue to care for the older
person. The counselor should tell the family that there will
be difficult times, such as admission day to the institution,
and that often on holidays and certain times of the day the
person may feel abandoned and forced to be there against
his will. Regular visits and planned activities with the older
person are crucial to his well-being and happiness.

The family is the key to adjustment of the elderly. They
can draw on great strengths within themselves, their relatives, their neighbors, and the Church to maintain an older
person at home.

Conclusion

"The meaning or lack of meaning that old age takes on in
any given society," writes Simone de Beauvoir, "puts the
whole society to the test, since it reveals the meaning or lack
of meaning of the entirety of life." Indeed, a society can be
judged by the way it treats its old. Certainly we will be judged
according to the commandment "Honour thy father and thy
mother." (Exodus 20:12.) The commandment "Thou shalt

love thy neighbour as thyself'" (Matthew 22:39) instructs us
to be concerned about other elderly people, not just about
family members. The Lord will work miracles as we serve
the elderly. He will hear our prayers and help us provide for
our own elderly and for others. Even though we may "cry
unto him in [our] houses . . . both morning, mid-day, and
evening," this is not all we must do: "For after ye have done
all these things, if ye turn away the needy, and the naked,
and visit not the sick and afflicted, and impart of your sub-
stance, if ye have, to those who stand in need—I say unto
you, if ye do not any of these things, behold, your prayer is in
vain, and availeth you nothing. and ye are as hypocrites who
do deny the faith. Therefore, if ye do not remember to be
charitable, ye are as dross, which the refiners do cast out, (it
being of no worth) and is trodden under foot of men." (Alma
34:21, 28-29.)

Let us not allow older people to enter old age with empty
hands. Let us strive to help them achieve respect and dignity
and to maintain this to the end of their lives.

SUGGESTED READINGS

Janet Brigham and Terry Mayer, "When Members Have Long-Term Needs," *Ensign* 9
   (July 1979): 10-13.

Brent D. Cooper, "We Adopted Some Grandparents," *Ensign* 11 (August 1981): 48-49.

William Fox, "Don't Call Me Old What's His Name," *Ensign* 9 (June 1979): 69.

Ron and Sheri Zirker, "Making Room for Grandpa," *Ensign* 11 (February 1981): 44-47.

ABOUT THE AUTHOR

Dr. J. Richard Connelly, associate director of the University of Utah gerontology
program, received his bachelor's and master's degrees in sociology from Brigham
Young University and his Ph.D. from Pennsylvania State University. He has taught
courses in human development, aging, child development, and family relations. He
has also been involved in the development and administration of gerontology programs at the University of Utah and Oregon State University and screening centers for
the elderly. Dr. Connelly is a consultant to state and private agencies and programs relating to retirement and care for adults and older people.

An author and lecturer, Dr. Connelly is a member of several professional and honorary organizations.

In the Church, Dr. Connelly has served in two bishoprics, as a stake Sunday School
president, and as a high councilor.

He and his wife, Cheryl Ann, are the parents of eight children.

17

Explaining Death to Children
Brent A. Barlow

Parents are one of the best sources from which children learn about the meaning of death. However, you may find yourself in a position where you must teach a child other than your own about death, or you may need to instruct the parents themselves.

Several years ago President Joseph F. Smith said, "Children are sure to be brought into some acquaintanceship with the incident of death, even during the kindergarten period; and it would be a great relief to the puzzled and perplexed conditions of their minds if some intelligent statements of the reason for death were made to them."[1]

It is evident from President Smith's statement and from daily observation of the Latter-day Saint child that the child is constantly learning about death. Many children's stories, at least in the original versions, have death themes, including "Snow White," "Little Red Riding Hood," and "The Three Little Pigs." In addition, some children's songs ("Rock-a-Bye Baby") and rhymes ("Humpty Dumpty") may be interpreted by children to contain death incidents. Contemporary children differ from children of previous generations in that many of them watch a great deal of television, which deals heavily with death and death-related incidents. Many children watch television about six hours every day, which is 50 percent more time than they spend in school. Watching television is the second largest activity in many children's lives, second only to sleep. On any given night (or day), a child can see several deaths on television. He may see literally hundreds and even thousands by the time he reaches adulthood. Questions are now being raised about the numerous, quick, synthetic, deaths children observe on television or in the movies. Tonight's villain is killed only to appear next week on another program in another role, thereby assuring the child that death is a temporary, emotionless event.

President Joseph F. Smith also observed:

> It is a principle widely accepted that it is not desirable to teach these little ones those things that are horrifying to childish natures. And what may be said of children is equally true in all stages of student life. But death is not an unmixed horror. With it are associated some of the profoundest and most important truths of human life. Although painful in the extreme to those who must suffer the departure of dear ones, death is one of the grandest blessings in divine economy; *and we think children should be taught something of its true meaning as early in life as possible.*[2]

It has recently been noted that children have differing views of death at certain age levels. In general, few children under the age of three have much comprehension of death, other than being separated. They are mostly concerned about someone caring for their physical, and to some degree emotional, needs. When children experience the death of a loved one, they need to be assured verbally and perhaps by touch that there are others who still love them and will care for them. Between the ages of about three and six, most children begin to understand death as a separation, but they often perceive it to be temporary or reversible, as when Prince Charming kisses Snow White and awakens her from her "sleep." Children during these ages can "kill" each other while playing cops and robbers because of the temporary nature of death. From the age of six to about eight or nine, children begin to understand the significance of death for others and the permanence of death during mortality. At about the age of nine, most children begin to realize the reality of their own death.

Several books and articles have recently been written with suggestions for explaining death to children. The following general guidelines have been condensed (and modified, in some instances) for use by Latter-day Saint parents:

1. Parents should explain that all living things die. This can be easily observed with plants, pets, or any living thing with which the child is acquainted.

2. Parents should discuss death with children before someone they love dies. Much of death education occurs after the event. It would be helpful for most children to discuss death not only when it occurs but also at a time when they are not experiencing the loss of a loved one.

3. Parents should explain the permanence of death as far as mortality is concerned. Although there have been instances where deceased parents or family members appeared as spirits to mortals, it would be questionable to teach children to anticipate such an event with any degree of certainty. Once someone dies, it is probable that we will not see that person again during this life.

4. Parents should use caution in making analogies about death. Telling a child, for example, that "Grandpa is taking a long journey" may be confusing, since people who go on long journeys often return. Also, telling a child that a dead person is asleep is objectionable because most sleeping people awake.

5. Parents should be careful in giving reasons for death. "Grandma died because she was sick" may be an inadequate answer, since it may cause an unrealistic fear of sickness. Not all sick people die. Saying, "He died because he went to the hospital" may cause undue fear of hospitals, and not all people who go to the hospital die. Another commonly given reason is, "Grandmother died because she was 'old.'" What is "old" to a child? It may be anyone fifteen years older than the child. A simple statement such as "Grandmother died because her body (or parts of it, such as her heart) ceased to function" may prove to be an adequate response to a child's inquiry as to "why Grandmother died." Parents should be honest, brief, and matter-of-fact in explaining death to children.

6. One of the most difficult aspects of death education is

explaining the theological implications of death. While our Heavenly Father could have been directly or indirectly involved in causing a death, and this belief may be consoling to an adult, it is often a difficult phenomenon for a child to understand. A son, for instance, may wonder why his father was "needed on the other side" when he may also have a great need for his father.

7. Children, particularly after age six or seven, should be allowed but not forced to participate in mourning and in the funeral. Children, as do others, need to work through their own grief and should be allowed, if they desire, to participate in the social and public ceremonies at the time of death. If a child at any age chooses not to participate in the funeral or public mourning, he should not be made to feel guilty or that he has "let the family down."

8. Parents should do all they can to alleviate any guilt a child may feel at the time of death. Many children feel responsible for a death because they acted "bad" and feel they are therefore being punished. If such feelings are carried to excess, such children may need professional attention. If a death, say of a grandparent, is equally difficult for all family members, parents may find it helpful to have another adult, a neighbor or relative, tend or be with the child during the early stages of bereavement or during the funeral so the child will not feel ignored.

9. Parents should discuss death with their children sometime after the children have experienced the loss of a loved one or a pet. By agreeing to discuss death again at another time, death education becomes a continuing process, not an isolated event.

10. Initially, parents should not discuss with children their own death or that of immediate family members. It would probably be more helpful at the beginning to have general discussions about death (1) as a normal process of life, (2) of all living things, and (3) of other people with whom the child is not so intimately or emotionally involved. Discussions of the child's death or that of parents, brothers, or sisters would best follow at other appropriate times.

11. Parents should explain to children that everyone has a body that eventually dies and a spirit that never dies. It is essential that children understand this as early as possible. Without such an explanation, it may be extremely confusing to a child to watch her deceased uncle being buried and then to be told, "Uncle Jim is now in heaven."

12. Parents should teach their children that there is a life after death and that they will someday be reunited with those they love.

13. Parents should teach their children the reality of the death and resurrection of Jesus Christ. President Joseph F. Smith stated:

> No explanation of death to a child's mind can anywhere be found that is more simple and convincing than is the death of our Master, connected as it is and ever must be with the glorious resurrection. . . . We are born that we may put on mortality, that is, that we may clothe our spirits with a body. Such a blessing is the first step toward an immortal body, and the second step is death. Death lies along the road of eternal progress; and though hard to bear, no one who believes in the gospel of Jesus Christ, and especially in the resurrection, would have it otherwise. Children should be taught early in life that death is really a necessity as well as a blessing, and that we would not and could not be satisfied and supremely happy without it. Upon the crucifixion and the resurrection of Jesus, one of the grandest principles of the gospel depends. If children were taught this early in life, death would not have the horrifying influence that it does have over many childish minds.[3]

NOTES

1. *Juvenile Instructor* 40 (June 1905): 336.

2. Ibid., italics added.

3. Ibid.

ABOUT THE AUTHOR

Dr. Brent Barlow, associate professor in the Department of Family Sciences at Brigham Young University, received his bachelor's and master's degrees from Brigham Young University and his Ph.D. from Florida State University. He has taught marriage and family classes at Florida State University; at Southern Illinois University, where he received the Outstanding Teaching Award; and at the University of Wisconsin—Stout, where he received the Distinguished Teaching Award. He writes a weekly column on marriage for the *Deseret News*, is the editor of *Understanding Death*, and has written two books on marriage, *What Wives Expect of Husbands* and *What Husbands Expect of Wives*, all from Deseret Book.

He is a member of the National Council on Family Relations, a member of the Association of Mormon Counselors and Psychotherapists, and a clinical member of the American Association for Marriage and Family Therapy.

Dr. Barlow has served in the Church as a Gospel Doctrine teacher, a branch president, a bishop's counselor, a high councilor, and a member of the Church curriculum committee that wrote *Foundations for Temple Marriage*, the manual used in temple preparation classes.

He and his wife, Susan, are the parents of six children.

18

What to Do When Someone Dies

Brent A. Barlow and Jolayne Wilson

How to Talk to a Dying Person

In talking to a dying person, a counselor should (1) take a genuine and compassionate interest in him; (2) listen to and try to understand him; and (3) try to get to know what he is like. In other words, a counselor should show genuine interest and concern in the person.

When talking to a dying person, a counselor should remember that he is also a living person; he has convictions, interests, hobbies, talents, and idiosyncrasies. The dying person is really no different than those who are well; in a sense, all of us are dying, but we just don't know the timetable. But those who *do* know frequently want to talk about their own illness and impending death.

If the person wants to talk about death, avoid talking about your own theological theories of death *unless they are asked for.* Be willing to listen to the person's own interpretation of what he is facing. As you talk to him, find out what he would like to do, now and in the future. Encourage him to share the decisions he is making. Decision-making is a sign of mental health. It means that the person is exercising some control over his life.

Children can often help a dying person remember that he is loved. Children are often uninhibited by our adult fears. Touch is an important part of helping a dying person, and children give touch without self-consciousness. (Unless the dying person has a contagious disease, he will do no harm to the child.)

After a Person Dies

Here is a checklist of matters to be taken care of after someone dies.

___ Contact bishop. Name: _____ .

___ Decide on time and place for funeral services.

___ Make arrangements according to your decision.

___ Make a list of family, colleagues, close friends, and employers to be notified by phone.

___ Notify each.

___ Purchase cemetery lot.

___ Decide on appropriate institutions to which gifts may be sent (if in place of flowers).

___ Write the obituary notice: include name, age, place of birth, cause of death, occupation, college degree, club memberships, military service, outstanding church and community work, survivors in the immediate family, time and place of service, selected memorial.

___ Deliver obituary to newspapers.

___ Identify insurance companies.

___ Notify them.

___ Identify lawyer or executor.

___ Notify each.

___ Check on will and safety deposit box. Location: _____ .

___ Arrange for close friends or family members to take turns answering the phone and the door, keeping a careful record of callers.

___ Arrange for necessary child care.

___ Coordinate supply and preparation of food for several days.

___ Consider special household needs—laundry, cleaning, preparations for family and guests—to be done by friends and neighbors.

___ Arrange other hospitality for visiting relatives.

___ Select pall bearers; select honor guards, when appropriate.

___ Notify them.

___ Arrange for disposition of flowers, if any, to area hospitals, rest homes, churches, weddings, shut-in friends.

___ Prepare a list of distant persons to be notified by letter or printed notice, and *delegate* notification responsibilities.

___ Send them.

___ Check current cash resources.

___ Check life and casualty insurance and death benefits, including Social Security, credit union, trade union, fraternal organizations, military benefits, and so on. Check also for income for survivors from these sources.

___ Check debts and installment payments. Some may carry insurance clauses. If there is to be a delay in meeting payments, consult with creditors and ask for time before payments are due.

Death sometimes creates stress and conflict in families. Decisions must be made, and family members often have differing opinions. Some of these stressful areas or topics are

1. Type of body disposition (burial, cremation, etc.)

2. Place of body disposition.

3. If there is a burial, should there be an open or closed casket?

4. Should mild sedatives be prescribed for survivors at the time of mourning to ease the pain and shock of the loss?

5. To what degree will children participate in the funeral or mourning rituals?

6. Should expensive jewelry (rings, watches, etc.) remain with the deceased?

7. When and in what manner will the estate or personal belongings of the deceased be transferred to the survivors? Who will be responsible for seeing this done?

These and other controverisal topics should ideally be discussed before the death of the family member or friend, and his suggestions should be considered in making these decisions.

How to Talk to the Bereaved

Following are suggestions of what one should avoid saying to the bereaved. Included are reasons why these phrases might be inappropriate.

"I've been through this myself." (The bereaved really aren't interested in anyone else's suffering at this time.)

"Death was a mercy." (How do we know if the death was a mercy. It may not be to the bereaved.)

"It was all for the best." (According to whom?)

"It was God's will." (We don't know if God wills everything.)

"You're young, you have your life ahead of you. There will be time for you to remarry," or "to have other children." (The person is not interested in those things at this time.)

"You know you're going to feel worse before you feel better." (That may be true, but they don't need you to tell them.)

"Don't cry about it; pray about it." (Tears can be a genuine expression of loss, and the bereaved may not feel like praying at that moment.)

"Others have had it worse." (Does that diminish their own sorrow?)

"You'll feel better next month." (The bereaved don't need this kind of cheering up.)

What could you say to the bereaved? Your presence alone communicates your concern, and often the best thing to do is just to listen, encourage the bereaved to talk, and reminisce with them. A handshake or embrace can also convey sympathy. You need not make a lengthy speech, but simply acknowledge the loss with statements like "I am sorry about John" or "I extend my sympathy." You could also share what the deceased means to you.

The Condolence Call

We are told in the Book of Mormon that we should be "willing to bear one another's burdens, that they may be light; yea, and . . . willing to mourn with those that mourn;

yea, comfort those that stand in need of comfort." (Mosiah 18:8-9.)

A condolence call is made soon after the person's death. It is a personal visit to the family of the deceased. There are many purposes for making a condolence call, including offering sympathy and help. Such a call should be made as soon as possible after receiving news of a death. It need not be long; fifteen minutes is often sufficient, unless the bereaved expresses a desire for a longer visit.

There are many different ways to express grief. Words are one way. Tears also convey feelings of grief. In fact, we should "weep for the loss of them that die." (D&C 42:45.)

The Condolence Letter

Sometimes you may be too far away to visit with the family, and in such cases a letter of condolence is appropriate. You may find such a letter hard to write, yet it is important to communicate your condolences. The following suggestions may help.

1. Consider why you are writing. Your letter is to reaffirm your relationship with the bereaved and to show you care. At the same time, it helps you accept the death.

2. Write and send the letter right away.

3. Consider alternatives besides a letter. If a letter seems too hard to write, pick up the phone and talk with the bereaved person. Or you may send a telegram.

4. A gift, such as a floral arrangement or a book, may bring you closer to those you feel concern for.

5. Be as personal as possible. Don't just send a printed card and sign your name. A handwritten note is best.

6. Be brief.

Sending another note to let the bereaved know of your continuing concern will help keep them from feeling abandoned, particularly several weeks after the funeral.[1]

Follow-up Visits

From James 1:27 we learn that "pure religion and undefiled before God and the Father is this, To visit the fatherless and widows in their affliction." Follow-up visits, as well as initial condolence calls and letters, are necessary after the funeral. It seems that when the funeral is over, the bereaved are forgotten. This should not be. Those who have lost a loved one need to know that they are still loved and have not been abandoned. Even when the bereaved have much sorrow they know who visits them. Your presence, even for a few minutes, lets them know that you are their friend and you have not forgotten them.

NOTE

1. Earl A. Grollman, *Concerning Death: A Practical Guide for the Living* (Boston: Beacon Press, 1974), pp. 282-86.

SUGGESTED READINGS

Brent A. Barlow, editor and author, *Understanding Death* (Salt Lake City: Deseret Book Co., 1979).

Douglas and Jewel Beardall, *Death and the LDS Family—Dealing with Death and Dying* (Provo, Utah: LDS Book Publications, 1979).

Paul H. Dunn and Richard M. Eyre, *The Birth That We Call Death* (Salt Lake City: Book-craft, 1976).

Earl A. Grollman, *Concerning Death: A Practical Guide for the Living* (Boston: Beacon Press, 1974).

Elisabeth Kübler-Ross, *On Death and Dying* (New York: MacMillan Publishing Co., 1969).

Spencer J. Palmer, *Deity and Death* (Provo, Utah: Brigham Young University Press, 1978).

ABOUT THE COAUTHOR

Jolayne Wilson, a graduate of Brigham Young University in family sciences, now resides in Salt Lake City.

19

Sexual Assault

Maxine Murdock

Sexual assault is a subject that is difficult for many people even to bring themselves to discuss. It is one thing to deal frankly with robbery, vandalism, and other forms of violence, but sexual crimes violate more then our pocketbooks and the orderliness of society; they strike at a part of the human soul that we think of as most intimate and personal—so much so that for some it may seem almost inappropriate to raise the issue.

Nevertheless, sexual assault is not a problem that can be wished away. It happens. Furthermore, it happens to Latter-day Saint women and children and is perpetrated by men who are Church members as well as by those who are not. We must face the problem and become aware of the *facts* so that we can understand how we can react in a constructive, supportive way when the crime happens to someone among us or is committed by someone among us.

The term *rape* has been defined in various ways. In all cases, however, rape is an exploitation and humiliation of an unwilling victim by a very personal invasion. Usually it is an attack by a stronger person against a weaker one. With the offense of child molestation, particularly in the case of incest, an adult is imposing his sexual desires and seeking gratification for himself by improper involvement with a child who has no way to defend herself or himself against an adult she or he may trust.

As a psychologist, I have talked with many women who

have been sexually molested recently, who were assaulted earlier in their lives, or who had been forced into incestual relationships at various ages and are still suffering the emotional trauma of their experiences. I have also counseled with men who have been accused or convicted of rape or sexual molestation. In my work, most of the recent rape victims I have seen reported that this abuse occurred on a date with a supposedly "fine" young man, often from their ward, whom they have dated at least several times. Rapes of this kind involve both verbal and physical coercion.

Perhaps a great proportion of sexually abused women I have seen have been earlier victims of incest. Incest is a major mental health problem that is only beginning to attract professional attention. According to the Harvard Medical School newsletter, between one-fourth and one-third of all girls nationwide will be sexually assaulted some time by an adult male, and about 10 percent actually have a sexual encounter with a relative. At least one percent become involved in father-daughter incest. Boys are less commonly molested within their families, but about 10 percent reportedly have had a sexual encounter with an adult, usually a male acquaintance rather than a relati .

In *every case* I have felt deeply the tragedy of the situation. Besides physically harming the victim, sexual crime degrades and humiliates her, and to the physical and severe psychological trauma are often added the person's tragically confused feelings as well. Many times I have listened to girls and women tearfully express the feelings resulting from their experiences—feelings of embarrassment, of having been shamed, and perhaps even of guilt for still being alive, for not losing their lives in a desperate, all-out counterattack. Sometimes the victims have horrible nightmares. One woman I counseled became terribly frightened whenever she realized she was alone—and this was twenty years after the event occurred. Under such circumstances, the victim feels a desperate need for support—support from her family, from Church leaders, from friends, and from ward members. Sometimes, however, this support is denied because of others' misunderstandings, and some have been, in effect, turned away to endure a solitary kind of hell. Fear of not receiving sympathetic understanding and support—or at least a fair hearing—is one reason so many instances of personal assault go unreported. Law-enforcement agencies and experts estimate that only about one-fifth (and perhaps as few as one-tenth) of all such crimes committed are actually reported to the police.

In my experience, much of our reluctance to understand and consequently to empathize with one who is a victim results from a number of mistaken ideas that are current in society. Following is a discussion of some of these myths or misunderstandings and their cost in human anguish. If you find yourself caught in any of the following misunderstandings about sexual molestation concerning either the perpetrators or victims, please reassess your own feelings before trying to help those desperately troubled women and children who have been victims or with those men who have committed such offenses.

Myth: Sexual assault doesn't happen to "nice" girls. There are several variations of this myth: Sexual assault happens "only to women with bad reputations" or "only to women from lower social classes." Furthermore, people often have a notion that sexual assault happens only to the young, the beautiful, or the provocatively dressed.

The truth is that *none* of these stereotypes are accurate. The victims come from every imaginable background. They are of every shape, race, and social class. They may be single or married, attractive or plain, dressed conservatively or stylishly, and have a variety of vocations. Their character and personal righteousness varies dramatically. They are of all ages—young, middle-aged, and old.

Included in this myth is the popular notion that if a woman is raped, she probably wanted it or invited it in some way. (Like most such myths, this one exists because of its convenience; it frees the nonvictim from having to care or trouble himself about the tragedy.) In fact, one young woman reported that a member of her ward remarked that any girl who was personally assaulted deserved it. He evidently felt that a woman always has control over the circumstances that can lead to personal assault.

The truth is that no child of God, young or old, *deserves* this experience, no matter what the circumstances. Furthermore, in most instances, the victim's dress or behavior could not in any way be interpreted as an invitation. Unfortunate incidents do sometimes occur because of misread social cues (especially among teenagers in their anxious and sometimes careless attempts to assume adult roles). For this reason, both men and women should be aware of the messages they might send by their clothing and behavior, and both men and women must be taught to regard each other with mutual respect. But the idea that a woman actually "asks for" or enjoys the kind of humiliating treatment that I read in the police reports and hear from the victims themselves—being threatened or coerced, even exposed to injury or death—is simply not true.

For very young girls (and sometimes boys) subjected to incest, sexual activity may become a regular part of their life, and only as they finally begin to interact with peers or become older do they begin to understand that something is wrong. Usually such cases of incest begin with fondling, which may feel good to a child. Then it gradually accelerates over several years before intercourse actually takes place.

Fortunately, many Church leaders in counseling positions are wonderful in their handling of members who have special need of love and support. But many, though sincere, may not have the understanding required or the experience to give all the support they could give. Sometimes their attitudes don't help the victims with the feelings they may be experiencing.

Myth: Sexual abuse occurs only in dark, deserted places and in disreputable neighborhoods. This erroneous idea is chiefly derived from television and the movies. While many such crimes do occur in secluded places, on dark streets, or in apartments and homes where windows or doors are left unlocked, and although statistically the majority of such crimes take place after dark (between 8:00 P.M. and 2:00 A.M.) and more frequently on weekends than at other times, they occur in almost every other setting as well. At least half of all such crimes are committed in the victim's home or apartment, most of them by men who know the victim—a neighbor, friend, date, relative, or other acquaintance. The tragic crime of incest almost always occurs in the person's home.

Myth: Rapists are shabby, lustful, and deranged psychopaths. Just as there is no typical rape victim, there is no typical rapist. They, too, vary in age, race, and social class. Some are married, others are single, and many have normal sexual relations with their wives. Some may appear shabby, while others may appear respectable. Some use verbal coercion and physical force; others use more subtle methods: "I'm a stranger in town. Could you show me the way to this address?" Sometimes strangers gain entry into a home or apartment by knocking at the door and giving a seemingly legitimate reason to enter. Some rapists plan their crime well in advance of the attack, having "cased" the scene beforehand. Others are simply opportunists who might see a woman at a stoplight or alone going toward her car and on impulse force her into a car. Drugs or alcohol or both are often involved.

In my counseling, I have talked to some psychopathic rapists who showed no emotion at all and who expressed neither concern nor hostility toward the victim. Some have expressed remorse for their actions. Some few are mentally retarded or have confused thinking due to psychotic or brain damage.

Most men who commit rape or who have learned deviant sexual patterns, however, are not deranged or seriously disturbed. They are men who have faulty attitudes toward sex or women. Theories abound as to why a rapist acts. Many are unable to establish loving relationships and use force to obtain gratification. Others want to exploit or humiliate. Some claim that their sexual drives get out of control under certain situations. Many have, for various reasons, become hostile toward all women; they commit their crime out of anger or to feel power and control. In addition to being a crime of passion, rape is a crime of violence.

Many rapists need to be confined in the interest of public safety, but most of them will be back in society in a few years, likely to repeat their crime unless they want to change and have received intensive and appropriate help.

Like those who commit rape, those who commit incestuous child molestation come from all social classes, geographic areas, and racial and religious backgrounds. The notion that incestuous fathers or stepfathers are all highly sexual and aggressive or have no sexual relationships with their wives is not true. Many are extremely conservative in their sexual beliefs and practices and have good sexual relationships with their wives. Families with a high risk of incest are often psychologically isolated with authoritarian fathers, passive mothers, and passive, obedient daughters. But incest occurs in all types of families. I have talked to many fathers and stepfathers who are incest offenders, as well as to several grandfathers, two of whom were involved with their granddaughters (both nine years old) and one who was involved with two of his grandsons. His first sexual experience with young boys, he reported, occurred years before when he was a youth leader.

Myth: Sexual abuse cannot happen to a woman against her will. Many women do resist rape successfully, but to state flatly that any woman can prevent personal assault if she really wants to is to ignore many of the circumstances that often surround crime.

First, the victim is usually smaller and considerably weaker than her male attacker. Often such crimes also involve weapons or coercion of some kind, and thus at least an implicit threat of injury or death (a small percentage of rapes do result in death, and at least a third result in injuries that require a physician's treatment). Finally, the victim is frequently taken by surprise and is paralyzed by fear—too terrified to make a sound, forgetting any preplanned strategies she may have had for resisting. And in any case, fighting or screaming that may discourage one rapist may motivate another.

While some attempted assaults may be averted by various means, many occur in spite of anything a woman might do. One woman described to me how she was held with a knife at her throat. Others have been choked into submission or unconsciousness by a much stronger assailant. Other women, tragically alone and helpless against an attacker or attackers, found that being assaulted was absolutely unavoidable. We must understand that even though a woman may have decided she would rather lose her life (probably an unwise decision) than be raped, she may very well *not* have this option.

Myth: The victim has lost her virtue. Virtue is something that cannot be taken away from anyone; it can only be given up voluntarily. If a person is robbed, the robber is held guilty and the victim seen as innocent. If someone takes a life, is the *victim* guilty of murder? Certainly not. And of course the same is true of rape: the guilt lies with the perpetrator, not with the victim.

Sadly, however, some people have tended to burden the rape victim with disgrace and subtle condemnation. More than one young woman has broken down and said to me, "Because of this, I'm not a virgin anymore." In almost every case, this becomes a terribly big issue as she tries to sort out her self-image following the crime. But a loss of virginity is not a loss of chastity where rape is involved. If a woman is robbed or mugged, she does not hesitate to report it to family and legal authorities, and she receives understanding, sympathy, and support from her friends, family, ward members, and Church leaders. But in the case of rape, she may wonder, "Will my husband (or boyfriend) forever think of me as unclean?" Unfortunately, some Latter-day Saint wives or girlfriends have been rejected in this way. I know of some tragic instances where innocent victims have actually been told, "No righteous Latter-day Saint man will ever want to marry you now." Sadly, others as well as the rapist can be brutal.

Certainly not all of the foregoing has been pleasant reading. Its purpose, though, has not been to dismay or alarm.
Instead, this review of common myths about personal assault is to persuade readers that any Latter-day Saint should
feel free to report sexual assault without being subjected to
more emotional injury. She should receive medical help in
case of physical disease or damage. She should receive psychological care or other understanding, supportive help so
that she can get over the agonizing psychic pain that is often
far more devastating than the actual physical trauma. And
she should be able to talk freely and with complete *confidentiality* with family members, Church leaders, friends, or
others who can provide compassionate and understanding
support. All who become involved must truly be non-
condemning, sympathetic, and assuring.

She can receive blessings and inspiration from the Lord
through righteous priesthood leaders. Fortunately, many of
the sisters I have talked to who were victims of rape or incest
have received marvelous support from Church leaders in this
regard. Few of us realize how serious and devastating the
trauma of assault can be. The impact on the soul is very
great, and the victim's need for blessings from others is also
very great. Here's where a priesthood leader or bishop can be
of outstanding help. Sometimes what the victim needs most
is to be listened to so that she can deal with her feelings instead of suppressing them.

Victims of child incest often are in a more difficult situation than are rape victims. While rape is traumatic, it is usually a one-time occurrence. But incest typically continues
over a period of years, frequently beginning when the girl is
five or six years old and persisting until she leaves home.
Physical force is seldom used, but verbal coercion and pressures to keep the experience secret are common. As one
father told me when questioned about why his daughter had
not objected, "She is an obedient child. She always does what
she is told." The victims sometimes have mixed feelings of
love for their fathers and guilt about their own involvement.
Many of them feel they are somehow to blame for their

father's behavior. One father who had been involved with his twelve-year-old stepdaughter told me in justifying himself, "She was so seductive! What did you expect me to do?" I suggested that it was his responsibility as an adult to say no. Another victim, who reported to her bishop an incestuous relationship with her father, expected that *she* would be excommunicated. The destructive psychological effects of incest often persist, and as adults, women frequently continue to suffer feelings of shame and stigmatization. They may have a low regard for themselves and have difficulty developing intimate relationships.

Following are some of the feelings many a victim of rape may experience.

1. She may seek to understand the meaning of what has happened; she may wish to talk repeatedly about her experience and resolve the question "What have I done to deserve this?" She may punish herself for some carelessness—for example, not checking to see if the windows were locked. Unfortunately, family, friends, or others may add chastisement for such errors—the kind of mistakes that probably all of us have made with no unfortunate consequences.

2. Guilt from the "if only" questions needs to be aired: "If only I had stayed home instead of going to the movie"; "If only I had gone to visit my sister when I thought I should"; "If only I had screamed instead of being so frightened I couldn't make a sound."

3. Other "why" questions need to be resolved: "Why did I park my car at the edge of the lot?" "Why did I stand around windowshopping until the stores had closed?" "Why did I go on a date with him?" "Why did I let him into my apartment?" Such questions are actually wishes to go back before the event. They are more "if only" questions than "why" questions. In a certain sense they have no answers, but a counselor can help a woman to understand her feelings through such questions, to look to the future and to find personal peace.

4. Feelings of being "used" or "unclean" (physically or

morally) or "unworthy of the love of a good man" need to be worked through and eliminated. In particular, the woman needs to resolve her feelings of hostility or despair and understand that these feelings do not have to be generalized to include all men.

Sadly, we often have the impression that we can sit down and *reason* with the victim, and that that kind of approach will do the whole job. Often, too, the victim will look at the situation in a reasonable way and say, "Yes, I was only a victim; I'm not really any different than I was before, and not all men are rapists." But at a deeper, emotional level, she will need much more time to resolve her feelings. Some victims reach an outward adjustment but carry deep-seated feelings with them for years, sometimes accompanied by a lingering bitterness and loss of hope that affects all areas of their lives.

5. Sometimes women have a delayed reaction to a rape or incestual relationship that has occurred much earlier in their lives. These reactions most often occur when a woman dates a young man she likes, but she discovers she cannot tolerate kissing or other appropriate physical contact. One approach I have found useful is to talk to the couple together explaining the likely reasons for the woman's feelings and having the man let the woman take the initiative, at least in the beginning, for any physical contact.

Incest victims may experience different feelings because their sexual involvement has usually been over a long period of time and has involved men they know and trust. Following are some of the feelings these young people have to deal with.

1. Mixed feelings of love and hate for the father or other close relative who has molested them.

2. Great anger for their helpless position or for the rationalizations given by the adult, such as "It is okay. It is our secret"; "It is my duty to show you what you do when you get married"; "I want you to learn about sex the right way"; and so on.

3. Feelings of guilt because they did not stop the adult or

guilt because the sexual stimulation was, in part, pleasurable. The young person must realize that the adult is almost always to blame.

4. Some incest victims develop a hypersexuality and may become sexually involved with peers. Or, to the contrary, they may generalize fear of sex to all men. They need help to understand their inappropriate feelings and behaviors.

5. If the incest has been reported by the victim and, because of this, the father or the child has been removed from the home, the family disruption is traumatic for all members, and particularly for the victim who may feel guilt for causing the conflict. Sometimes she may wish she had never revealed the problem to anyone because of the disruption it has caused. She needs reassurance that her action was correct.

Helping a victim of sexual assault is complex and may take much time and involve both ecclesiastical leaders and professional counselors. However, with proper support and help, a victim *can* resolve her problems and live a happy life with normal relationships. But for this to occur, a woman needs first to accept herself as a worthy person. She must place blame where it belongs—on the sexual offender—and not place the blame on herself. She must realize that she has not lost her virtue, that she has no sin that requires confession or repentance, and that she is just as acceptable to an understanding boyfriend or husband, to Church leaders, and to God, as before.

ABOUT THE AUTHOR

Dr. Maxine Murdock, clinical psychologist at the Brigham Young University Counseling Center, received her bachelor's and graduate degrees at that same institution. Having a Ph.D. in clinical psychology, Dr. Murdock does part-time counseling in private practice and part-time counseling with the Utah State Prison System.

Dr. Murdock has held numerous callings in the Church, including stake Primary and Relief Society presidencies and many teaching positions.

She is the mother of three married children.

20

Child Abuse: Counseling the Abusive Parent

Lynn M. Jacobson

He took it and bit it to see if it was good, and then he said he was going down to get some whiskey; said he hadn't had a drink all day. When he got out of the shed, he put his head in again and cussed me for putting on frills and trying to be better than him; and when I reckoned he was gone he came back and put his head in again and told me to mind about that school because he was going to lay for me and lick me if I didn't drop that. . . . The Judge and the widow went to law to get the court to take me away from him and let one of them be my guardian; but it was a new judge that had just come, and he didn't know the old man; so he said courts mustn't interfere and separate families if they could help it; and he'd druther not take a child away from its father. So Judge Thatcher and the widow had to quit on the business.

—Mark Twain, Huckleberry Finn

It was two o'clock when Susan finally sat down with the book she had begun two weeks ago. Three-year-old Marie was quietly playing in her room, and Johnny was at school. Feeling exhausted and annoyed for having so little time to herself, Susan sighed and reopened the book to page one. In this quiet moment, Susan was almost relaxed. But her bliss was short-lived. First there was a bang, then a crash. Susan jumped up and ran into the dining room. Marie was sitting in the middle of what remained of her best vase, broken into tiny pieces. Susan was furious. She was a loving and dedicated parent, but she lost all of the inner controls that loving parents have, and she hit Marie and did not stop hitting her.

Later, Susan was numb and sick inside at the sight of the heavy bruising on Marie's body.

From the time Huck Finn sought refuge on a Mississippi raft from an abusive father to the more contemporary case of Susan and Marie, there have no doubt been millions of child-abuse victims. Even though many of our most tender emotions are for our children, child abuse has always existed and has now become a serious social problem. The causes are the same today as they were for Huck Finn, but they are now probably even more pervasive.

Because child abuse and neglect usually occur in the privacy of the home, no one really knows how many children are affected. Child abuse must be discovered and reported before the child can be protected, and there is general agreement that this does not happen in most abuse incidents.

The National Center on Child Abuse and Neglect estimates that approximately one million children are abused by their parents each year. Of these children, as many as one hundred thousand to two hundred thousand are physically abused; sixty thousand to one hundred thousand are sexually abused, and the rest are neglected. Each year more than two thousand children die in circumstances suggestive of abuse or neglect.[1]

Although children have always been abused and neglected, until recently the problem was considered only in terms of individual cases—people knew that "the fellow down the block is pretty hard on his kids" without realizing that he had thousands of companions. Not until the "battered child syndrome" was defined in 1962 was significant attention focused on the problem. It ranks as one of the greatest risks to the health of children. The problem is difficult to define and to assess and is extremely challenging to deal with.

Definition of Neglect and Abuse

An abused child has been defined by statute as "a child

whose physical or mental health or welfare is harmed or threatened with harm by acts of the child's parent or other person responsible for the child's welfare." A more workable definition for the lay counselor may be: "A child who is repeatedly mistreated or neglected by parent or other guardian, resulting in injury or harm."

Counseling the Abusive Parent

When counseling with abusive parents, it is important to be aware of reporting laws. These laws vary from state to state, but almost all states have some type of reporting law. Such laws usually require *mandatory reporting* of suspected cases of child neglect and abuse to the local police or social service office. The lay counselor should be aware of the reporting laws of his state to assure compliance with the law. Utah law, for example, requires mandatory reporting to the local police or Children's Protective Services by anyone, including physicians, religious counselors, dentists, police, nurses, school counselors and teachers, and so on, who has reason to believe that a child has been subjected to mistreatment or abuse. The lay counselor also has a moral responsibility to see that child abuse is reported to the appropriate agency. By law, a person cannot be held liable for reporting in good faith a suspected case of neglect or abuse.

The lay counselor should be able to recognize the need for professional help and not become overly involved in complex behavior problems. His primary obligation is to recognize the existence of the problem and take the necessary steps to insure the safety of the children involved. In cases where a child's health and safety are in jeopardy, the counselor should immediately contact the local Child Protection Agency. Many child protection agencies have twenty-four-hour hotlines.

The lay counselor can best help abusive parents by giving support and compassion. Honoring reporting requirements is both responsible and compassionate. It offers a chance for parents to change as well as protection for the child. To deal with the complex, underlying causes of the abuse, professional counselors should be contacted.

Many parents may request help in dealing with their inability to control themselves while disciplining their children. They may admit to "going too far" or may fear that they will not control their anger in the future. In such instances of isolated minor abuse or fear of possible abuse, it is important for the counselor to establish with the parents at the beginning of counseling that he is required by law to report certain acts, but that he will help within certain limitations. If an abusive act is reported that does require reporting to the Child Protection Agency, the counselor should emphasize that the agency will be supportive and helpful. Most parents fear they will lose their children if a government agency is involved. However, every effort is made to protect the child and to maintain the family unit. Only when a child's immediate health and safety are at risk is the child temporarily placed outside of his own home.

The lay counselor can usually support families who are already involved in professional counseling or families in which neglect or abuse is only threatened or minor.

Understanding the reasons for the abuse is critical for counselors. Often the abuse is a reaction to problems or stresses with which the parents do not cope. The abusive act is seldom premeditated or intentional, and abusive parents almost always love their children. Most such parents are normal, and few are criminals or are mentally unbalanced. Every parent, under certain circumstances, has the potential to abuse a child.

Often the abusive behavior is not the real problem but is symptomatic of some serious difficulty in the parents' or the family situation.

Below are several common factors associated with child abuse, along with some suggestions on how to counsel families affected by these factors.

Factors Related to Child Abuse
1. *Immaturity*. Very young, insecure parents often cannot understand their child's behavior or needs.

2. *Lack of parenting knowledge.* Some parents do not know the various stages of child development.

3. *Unrealistic expectations.* Parents expect their children to behave like miniature adults.

4. *Social isolation.* Parents might not have family or friends to help with the heavy demands of small children.

5. *Unmet emotional needs.* Parents who cannot relate well with other adults may expect their children to satisfy their need for love, protection, self-esteem, and so on.

6. *Poor childhood experiences.* Many abusive parents were mistreated themselves as children.

7. *Frequent crises.* Because of financial problems, loss of employment, legal problems, major illness, and so on, a parent may "take it out" on the child.

8. *Drug or alcohol problems.* Chronic drug or alcohol abuse limits parents' ability to properly care for their children.[2]

Possible Solutions

Effective listening skills are critical to the assessment of any problem. The counselor should let the parent present the problem without interruption other than encouraging comments or occasional clarifying questions. This initial description of the problem will help the counselor determine whether he should proceed with counseling or refer the family for professional help.

The counselor should accept the parent as a troubled person who needs help rather than labeling him as a "child abuser." However, accepting the person does not mean the counselor accepts his behavior. He should make clear to the parent that this is the case. He should develop a relationship with the parent in which there is free expression and discussion of feelings without the threat of rejection.

The counselor should help the parent deal with his specific problems. The degree of his motivation to change is an important factor in helping him. If the parent recognizes the existence of the problem and is reaching out for help, the possibility of change is good. The counselor should not hesitate to use other resources in the community, ward, or neighborhood when this can be done without violating the confidentiality of the relationship.

With a knowledge of some of the common causes of child abuse, the counselor should be able to design a counseling program for the family. Many parents will benefit immensely just from having a caring person to talk with. Such support can come from visiting teachers, home teachers, a nurse, a homemaker, nutritional aides, relatives, or close friends.

How the counselor handles the initial request for help will in large measure determine the effectiveness of his counseling with the family. The counselor should reach out to the abusive parents with sympathy for them as troubled people. Still, all counseling should first protect the child and secondly maintain and support the family whenever possible.

NOTES

1. National Center on Child Abuse and Neglect, Children's Bureau; Administration for Children, Youth, and Families; Washington, D.C.

2. *What Everyone Should Know about Child Abuse*, State of Utah Department of Social Services, 150 West North Temple, Salt Lake City, Utah 84110.

SUGGESTED READINGS

Felix P. Biestek, *The Casework Relationship* (Chicago: University of Chicago Press, 1957).

Vincent J. Fontana, *Somewhere a Child Is Crying* (New York: MacMillan Publishing Co., 1973).

Joseph Goldstein, Anna Freud, and Albert J. Solnit, *Beyond the Best Interests of the Child* (New York: Free Press, 1973).

C. Henry Kempe and Ray E. Helfer, eds., *The Battered Child*, 3rd ed. (Chicago: University of Chicago Press, 1980).

C. Henry Kempe and Ray E. Helfer, eds., *Helping the Battered Child and His Family* (Philadelphia: J.B. Lippincott Co., 1972).

ABOUT THE AUTHOR

Lynn M. Jacobson, protective services worker for the Utah Division of Children, Youth, and Families, received his bachelor's degree from Brigham Young University and his master of social work degree from the University of Utah. He has worked in his present professional assignment for over twelve years.

In the Church, he has held various teaching positions.

He and his wife, Sharon, are the parents of five children.

21

Teaching Young People about Morality

Todd Parker

If a person were to ponder the question "What is God's greatest power?" would not a plausible answer be "His power to create"? And if a second question were posed, "What is his finest creation?" would not the answer be "His children"? For he has said that his work and glory is "to bring to pass the immortality and eternal life of man." (Moses 1:39.) This being the case, God must consider creative power good, most sacred, and something to be treated with great respect. Is it any wonder, then, that he has decreed that the misuse of this power is "most abominable above all sins save it be the shedding of innocent blood or denying the Holy Ghost?" (Alma 39:5.)

When a person finds himself in a position to teach someone about this power, he must do so with the utmost care. A teacher or counselor must have a deep reverence for this power and an ability to communicate the eternal importance of its correct use. This process and power is eternal. Brigham Young stated, "[God] created man, as we create our children; for there is *no other process of creation* in heaven, on the earth, in the earth, or under the earth, or in all the eternities, that is, that were, *or that ever will be.*" (*Journal of Discourses* 11:122; italics added.) This process and power, which had no beginning and will never end, is something that should be discussed carefully and prayerfully with respect for its eternal nature.

Those who abuse this power through adultery, promis-

cuity, or other sexual sins will lose the opportunity for its use
in eternity. (See D&C 131:4.) Alternatively, if a person properly uses this power during his mortal probation, keeping
the laws and ordinances of the gospel, he may be granted its
use for eternity.

Teaching sexual morality should be grounded on correct
principles and have a scriptural basis. Because many people
involved with moral transgression feel the weight of their sin
and find it embarrassing, awkward, or shameful to discuss,
we will here consider some important principles to help
them.

Avoiding and Overcoming Temptation

The Savior has given us great counsel in the Sermon on
the Mount. Jesus first discusses the key to the problem in
Matthew 5:28, where he states, "Whosoever looketh on a
woman to lust after her hath committed adultery with her
already in his heart." The problem is one of controlling the
mind. The body will not respond or engage in sin unless the
mind dictates it first. Therefore, if the mind were controlled,
so also would be all moral transgression. But the Savior does
not stop with just this insight; in verses 29 and 30 he gives us
the key to shunning all sexual temptations: "If thy right eye
offend thee, pluck it out, and cast it from thee . . . and if thy
right hand offend thee, pluck it out, and cast it from thee."
The admonition to "pluck out the eye" or to "cut off the
hand" should not be separated from verse 28, where the
problem of lust is discussed.

If we substitute the word "tempt" for "offend" in verses
29-30, the meaning becomes more apparent. If something
tempts you through your eyes, whether it be television,
movies, or pornography, you should "pluck out" or remove
your eye from whatever it is that tempts you. Notice that the
Savior says to "cast it from thee," meaning to get your eye as
far from the tempting situation as you can. If the eye does
not view it, the mind will not dwell upon it; lust will not
occur, and the action will not follow.

Often, however, when the eye is not "plucked out" and the mind is permitted to dwell on unclean thoughts, then the hands become involved in the transgression. By commanding that we cut off our hand if it is "offended" or "tempted," the Savior again is simply saying, "If you are tempted to do things or touch things with your hands that you shouldn't, remove yourself from that situation."

The Savior's plea is to control our circumstances. We are to remove ourselves from tempting situations and cast ourselves far enough from them that our curiosity is not stirred toward sinful acts.

Joseph of Egypt was lured into a tempting situation by Potiphar's wife. She tempted him "day by day," but "he hearkened not unto her, to lie by her, *or to be with her.*" (Genesis 39:10, italics added.) Joseph knew if he didn't "pluck himself out" by not even being around her, he might begin to entertain the temptation. When Potiphar's wife attempted to seduce Joseph by clutching him, he "fled, and got him out." (Genesis 39:12.) Joseph didn't run because of cowardice, but because he understood the principle: "Can a man take fire in his bosom, and his clothes not be burned?" (Proverbs 6:27.) One who remains near a tempting situation is probably going to be affected. The only proper course of action is to remove oneself from the situation. Preferably, one would never get into it in the first place.

King David provides us with a negative example of this principle. Finding it too hot to sleep one evening, he went for a walk. He noticed his neighbor's wife, Bathsheba, bathing. David did not immediately "pluck out his eye." He tarried and let Satan, using curiosity and allurement, trap him. David then invited Bathsheba to see him. This only increased the temptation, and adultery was the result. David then arranged for the murder of Bathsheba's husband. David, a king, a prophet, who killed Goliath with a sling and wrote the beautiful twenty-third psalm, had "fallen from his exaltation." (D&C 132:39.) Why? Ultimately because "at the time when kings go forth to battle . . . David tarried still at

Jerusalem." (1 Samuel 11:1.) What was David's mistake? He
was in the wrong place at the wrong time. Many people,
young and old alike, have committed sexual transgressions
because of similar circumstances; they were in the wrong
place at the wrong time.

Following is an excerpt from a letter by one such young
lady. She had become pregnant as a junior in high school.
She married and moved away. She then wrote the following
to her seminary teacher:

> Dear Brother _____,
>
> I guess you are a little surprised at hearing from me. How are
> things with you? . . . I am sorry I didn't write sooner but I guess you
> could say I really didn't have the guts. . . .
>
> You can tell your seminary kids that you do *not* have to be inactive
> or rotten to the core to mess up. And it doesn't always happen to
> somebody else. All you've got to do is *be in the wrong place at the
> wrong time.* It's really simple to do that. Nor do you fall all at once,
> but just a little bit at a time. Please tell them the importance of not
> moving one little inch off the place where they know they should
> stay. Once you move an inch it's a lot easier to move a foot, and once a
> foot, a yard, etc. . . . Believe me, it's a long road back.

Inviting Someone to Change Behavior

Too often people feel that they are too entangled in sin to
change. The future looks hopeless. It is true that "where
there is no vision, the people perish." (Proverbs 29:18.) The
responsibility of a teacher or counselor is to give new perspectives, new alternatives, new approaches, and new insights into controlling one's behavior—hence new vision.
The second half of Proverbs 29:18 reads, ". . . but he that
keepeth the law happy is he." The person seeking to change
must be convinced that keeping the law brings more happiness than breaking the law.

How does one convince another person that he can stop
sinning? First, let him understand what Paul said about
temptation: "God is faithful, who will not suffer you to be
tempted above that ye are able; but will with the temptation also make a way to escape, that ye may be able to bear
it." (1 Corinthians 10:13.)

Often one who says, "I can't stop the sin" is really saying, "I don't know how" or "I don't want to." In either case, the attitude must be given up if change is to occur.

He must be taught in modern terms what the Savior meant when he said to "pluck out the eye" or "cut off the hand." An example of this may be a young man who believes that he cannot control his passion while with his girlfriend. He may be picturing the two of them alone watching the late movie. But if he pictured himself playing Monopoly with her and her family, he may realize that he could control his behavior under those circumstances and so could control it when they were alone. The thought is father to the act.

The chart on the next page may be useful in helping young people see how to control their behavior. Actually, nothing on the chart is magic. It will not "work" on them; they must "work" on it. In this way they can learn to control their feelings and behavior.

To understand the terrible price a person pays for sin, it is often helpful for him to make a price list of the "cost" of sin. A typical price list (a list of the consequences of sin) follows:

Sin: Necking and petting

Prices I am paying to continue my behavior:
1. I feel guilty.
2. I am grouchy with my family.
3. My grades are falling in school.
4. I never get excited about anything else anymore.
5. Things that used to interest me seem boring.
6. We always fight about necking and petting.
7. I feel out of place at church.
8. I'm getting further away from my parents and brothers and sisters.
9. I don't feel like I'm part of anything.
10. My appetite is gone. Food tastes lousy.
11. I'm losing some good friends.
12. I feel everyone stares at me in seminary and in church.

Moving Away from Temptations

Inappropriate Behavior	Removing the Tempting Situation
1. Having lustful thoughts	1 a. Never dwell on the sensual but quickly replace a bad thought with a good one. Carry cards containing scriptures or words to hymns. When the improper thought enters the mind, concentrate on memorizing from the card.
b. Never allow your eyes to dwell on any tempting material. Be as Joseph, who "got him out." Either turn away or leave immediately.
c. Maintain good friends and company who also desire to avoid temptation.
d. Never purchase or wear anything immodest.
2. Reading pornography	2 a. Never be alone where the pornography is. Don't even get close enough to see the cover.
b. Do not dwell on or speculate about what may be in it. (Use 1a if necessary.)
c. If you have pornography, fortify yourself while away from it and then get rid of it. Burn it. Destroy it. Make it irretrievable.
d. Make a commitment to a friend that you will report to him if you are ever tempted to read pornography.

3. Necking and petting

   3 a. Never steady date until the young man has fulfilled a mission. In some cases, it's easier for young people if a parent plays the role of the "bad guy" who enforces this rule.

     b. Never be alone together for extended lengths of time.

     c. Always have an activity where the focus is something other than just the two of you together.

     d. Agree never to park, watch television alone, and so on.

     e. See 4d and 4f.

4. Fornication and adultery

   4 a. Never be alone together in an apartment, house, or other place where intercourse could occur.

     b. Never take off or even undo your clothes.

     c. Do not engage in conversations about anything that would cause arousal.

     d. Never try to "see how strong you are."

     e. Don't be so foolish as to say you will only neck and pet but not go any further.

     f. Remember President Kimball's words: "No man or woman has the right to cause arousal in anyone but his or her spouse."

13. We never do anything fun anymore—we always just "make out."
14. Our respect for each other is diminishing or gone.
15. I have doubts and fears about being worthy to go to the temple.
16. I feel awful about always avoiding the bishop—never looking him in the eye.

Young people (as well as adults) need to know that they can control their behavior and that there is a price for sin. They also need to recognize that when their lives are filled with meaningful activities, the temptation to transgress is smaller. Motives make a considerable difference in one's ability to control behavior. Self-control results from a foundation of clear-cut goals, beliefs, and activities. Personal growth comes not only from thinking (study) but also from doing. As you teach a young person self-control, you might also suggest meaningful activities such as the following: service in a hospital, rest home, public library, or school; helping a widow, a shut-in, or a handicapped person; reading to the blind; teaching children a skill; participating in church, community, or school sports programs; engaging in high adventure activities such as hang gliding, skiing, flying, and racing, which teach self-control, endurance, and self-confidence. Carefully chosen reading materials, such as biographies of great people, help anyone to understand that growth comes through discipline and sacrifice. Encourage youth to accept leadership positions that require them to be an example and in which they must exert themselves to teach others. Help them to measure their growth in some area of life—music, writing, athletics, woodworking, or other hobbies. Encourage them to pray daily, to study the scriptures, to read inspiring articles or books, and to serve in the Church.

If it seems appropriate, you might help the young person develop a plan to help in his progress. The plan might include such things as these:

1. A daily schedule (leaving no time where the sin may result).

2. A chart showing each day the sin is not committed and each day planned activities are followed.

3. Periodic interviews with the bishop.

4. Scripture study outline.

5. A goal to make prayers longer and more meaningful.

Goal-setting is important, but evaluation of progress is a necessity. Moreover, the person seeking help must specify what his own actions will be and set his own goals. People lose hope if they feel they aren't progressing, and we all love to be rewarded for our efforts. Something as small as a calendar with a check for each day of appropriate behavior works well. Help the person learn that the longer he goes without sin, the stronger and more able he will be to resist.

In Conclusion

The Lord has said, "The worth of souls is great in the sight of God." (D&C 18:10.) How much is one soul worth to the Father? The price paid to save that soul was the life of the Savior. We, too, must realize the great worth of each soul we counsel. In so doing, we will be better able to help that soul avoid and overcome the ruinous effects of immorality.

ABOUT THE AUTHOR

Todd Parker holds a bachelor's degree in English from Weber State College and a master of education degree in counseling and guidance from Brigham Young University. A doctoral candidate in Educational Psychology at BYU, he resides in Orem, Utah, where he teaches seminary at Orem High School. Before coming to Utah, he taught seminary and adult religion classes in Mesa, Arizona. He has also taught at various education weeks and youth conferences. In the Church, he has served in various callings with young people and as an elders quorum president. He and his wife, Debbie, have four children.

Index

θ